For University Federal,

With best wishes,

March '03

The Gift of Community

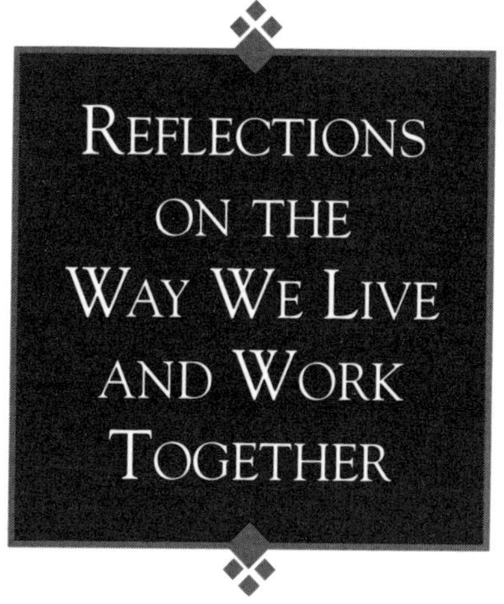

Gary D. McCaleb

The Gift of Community: Reflections on the Way We Live and Work Together

1648 Campus Ct.
Abilene, TX 79601
www.hillcrestpublishing.com

Cover Design and Typesetting by Sarah Bales

Printed in the United States of America

ISBN 0-89112-426-8

Library of Congress Card Number: 2001096089

1,2,3,4,5

ACKNOWLEDGEMENTS

This book represents the completion of a project that began as an idea more than ten years ago.

Many citizens of Abilene, Texas played a role in this book. Had it not been for the rewarding experience of living among such a wonderful group of people and for the enlightening opportunity to serve as mayor, I doubt I would have undertaken this project. Many more people should be acknowledged by name than can be listed here. There has also been an "attitude of anonymity" that has often prevailed—in the spirit of true volunteerism many of those who have done much for our community have done so without interest in attention or recognition. I am grateful to each one who has helped me see what is valuable—and possible—in community.

Several years ago, Glenn Dromgoole, then editor of the *Abilene Reporter-News*, invited me to write a weekly column for the paper. Absent that experience, I am doubtful that I would have ventured into this project; some of those columns were seeds for ideas in this book. Thank you, Glenn.

Three of the "reflections" were first developed as speeches for the Texas Historical Society, the Texas Tourism Council, and the Advisory Board of the National League of Cities. I am grateful for the opportunity they provided and the thoughts their invitations provoked.

Over the years, there have been a series of people who were a part of the office "team" who provided important input, assistance, and encouragement that was vital and appreciated. For all they did, I am grateful to Suzanne Allmon, Sharon Johnston Epps, Paulette Haught, LeeAnna Ladyman, Kathy

Horner, and Jennifer Ham.

As the publication date and deadlines loomed, some very special people played prominent roles in the final stages. Julia Johnson Russell, Kelly Shunk Speck, Yvette Cantu and Monica Guerrero served as excellent research assistants. Lea Watkins did a masterful job of coordinating the project, putting all the pieces together, and "getting it right."

After turning the manuscript over to the publisher, it had the good fortune to fall into the hands of Karen Cukrowski, a skillful editor, whose deft and sensitive touches were sincerely appreciated.

Last, I especially want to thank my wonderful personal community: my wife Sylvia, most of all; Cara Lee and Brad; Bryan and Dana; and the grandkids, Lindsay, Caleb, Riley, Maggie, and Colton. I am so grateful for your patience, cooperation, understanding, support, and love. I'm thankful to enjoy the benefits of such a great miniature of community.

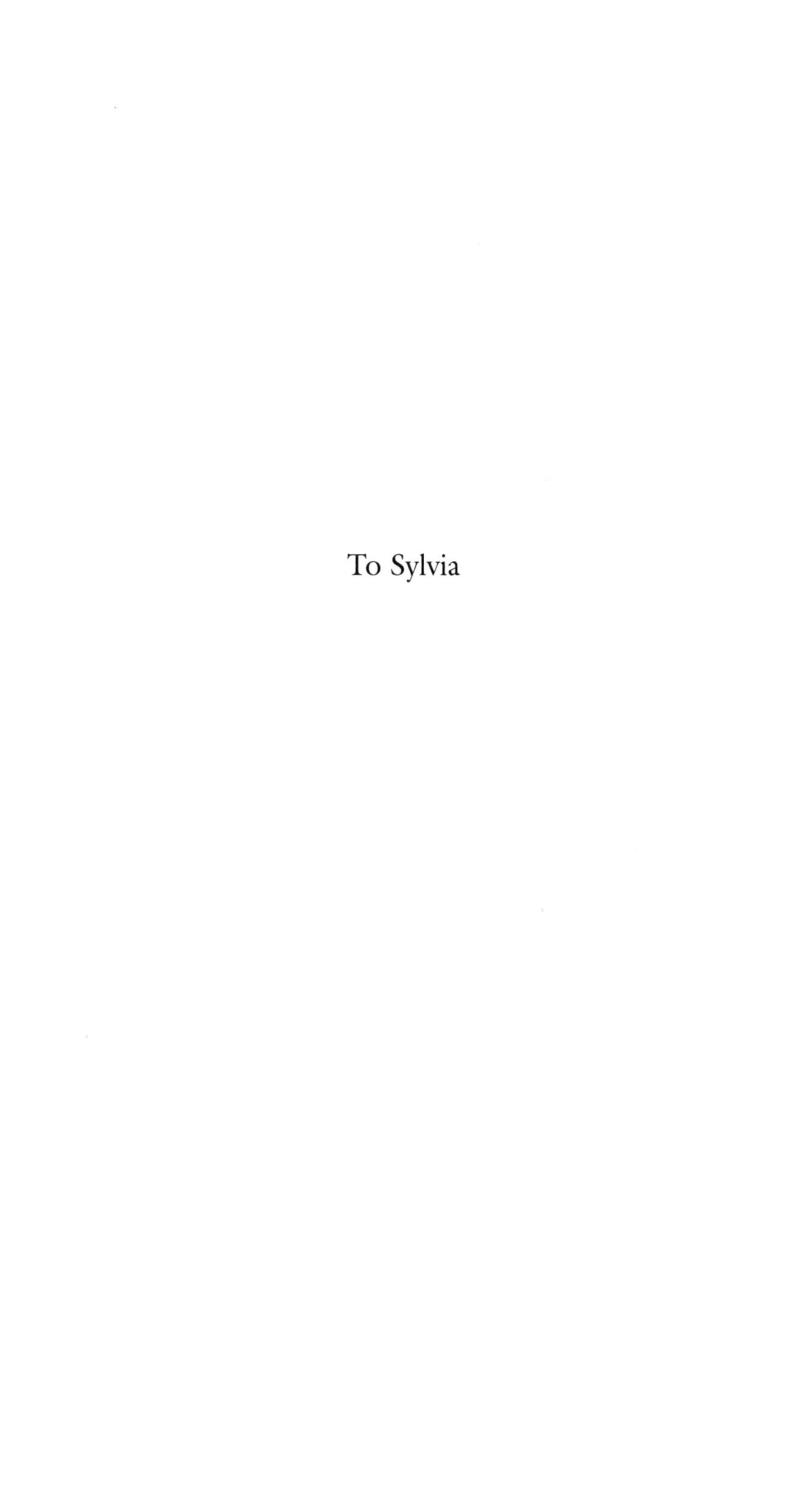

To Sylvia

Table of Contents

❖

A NOTE ABOUT THE STRUCTURE OF THE BOOK:

1. The sources which I consulted or quoted are referenced at the back of the book, organized by section heading;
2. The reader will find a list of the cities I mention at the back of the book; these, too, are organized by the sections in which they are found; and
3. Each section provides an introduction to the reflections which follow.

Introduction

My wife and I have lived in Abilene, Texas for more than thirty-five years. It's the place we call home. We think it has been a good place to live, work, and raise a family.

For nine years I had the honor of serving as Mayor of Abilene. During those years, I enjoyed a unique perspective from which to watch "how a city works." In 1999, I decided not to run for a fourth term for mayor and instead accepted the opportunity to establish and direct a Center for Building Community at Abilene Christian University. My primary hope was to have more time to study and understand "how community works."

The more I studied the situation, the more I became convinced that it was helpful to me to use two lenses to view Abilene—one for the city, the other for the community. In my mind they represented two very different concepts. The "city" represented that which was tangible and measurable—the steel, asphalt, and concrete. The "community" represented the intangible, the invisible, that which is difficult, if not impossible to measure—respect, trust, and compassion.

Both "city" and "community" are important. Both must be given attention by concerned citizens, elected officials, and non-elected leaders. But it seems that we pay far more attention to the "city" issues than to the issues of "community"—and probably there are some reasons for that, such as: (1) It's easier to tend to the seen than the unseen; (2) It's easier to measure progress in the "seen" than the "unseen"; (3) It's easier to make rules and pass ordinances related to the "city" than the "community"; and (4) The "city" issues may be less personally sensitive than "community" issues.

In general, I am concerned about the health of "community" in our cities—and elsewhere. I believe that for the same reason a "spirit of community" is important to a city, it is also important to a business, university, hospital, church, or any other structured organization of a group of people.

In general, I like to think that what we are trying to do at the Center for Building Community is to find better ways to identify and nurture the forces that can bring us together so that they will always be stronger than the forces at work that would drive us apart.

The reason the book is titled *The Gift of Community* is because I am convinced that any "sense of community" we enjoy comes as a result of the charitable spirit and generous nature of others.

That has certainly been true here in Abilene. Over and over during my years as mayor, as well as before and since, I witnessed great generosity from my fellow citizens—gifts of money—yes, as in the case of our downtown revitalization—but also great gifts of time, talent, ideas, and affection.

We can budget for great structures of steel and concrete, but no one can purchase community. It can only be realized as a result of people who care enough to give of themselves to that very special cause called community.

"The only gift is
a portion of thyself."
- Emerson

A Sense of Community

Conrad Hilton came to oil-crazed West Texas in 1919, searching for a place to launch his career. He was looking for a bank to buy when he walked into a two-story red brick building in Cisco, Texas—a building he later described as "a cross between a flophouse and a gold mine."

In his autobiography, *Be My Guest*, he recalls developing one of the principles that has "been basic in every one of my subsequent operations from Waco to Istanbul." Shortly after assuming ownership of his first "Hilton Hotel," he assembled his twenty or so employees to explain the importance of their work: "You're the only ones who can give smiling service," he said. "Clean rooms, spotless halls, plenty of fresh soap and linen. Ninety percent of the hotel's reputation is in your hands." That first hotel in Cisco is no longer operational, but today there are over 500

Hilton Hotels "from Waco to Istanbul."

A few years ago I attended a conference at the Irvine Hilton in California. A widely publicized national campaign called "Hilton's Million-Dollar-A-Day Thank You" was underway. While checking out, I was presented with three gift coupons—one for each night stayed in the hotel. On each coupon were the words, "Please accept this gift as a token of our appreciation."

But the positive feeling I had about my stay at the Irvine Hilton was influenced by three personal encounters more than by the three coupons.

Encounter One: After an early morning jog, I returned to my fifth-floor room. As I stepped out of the elevator and headed down the quiet hallway, the silence was suddenly broken with the words, "Good Morning, Sir!" Turning around, I discovered a hotel employee was speaking to me. He was delivering room service breakfast and had suddenly appeared out of another hallway. Walking behind me on the carpeted hallway, he could have let me go quietly into my room—but he didn't.

Encounter Two: Elevator rides can at times be the most prized form of transportation. When hundreds of delegates are operating on the same daily schedule, the congested conditions can rival the Los Angeles freeways. When I turned the corner to the four elevators, I saw the doors of elevator number one slowly closing—if only I had arrived five seconds earlier.

Then, almost mysteriously, the doors opened again. As I entered the elevator, I discovered a bellboy who had seen my reflection in the metallic strips of the elevator door, even though I hadn't seen him. He could have let me wait for the next elevator—but he didn't.

Encounter Three: When checking out at the end of a conference, it's not unusual to find long lines with everyone in a hurry and no one in a pleasant mood on either side of the counter. But this time it was different.

Upon reaching the cashier's desk, I met a pleasant young lady with the name "Leticia" pinned to her jacket. She handled the paperwork in an efficient manner, and my business was completed quickly. I then stepped aside, making way for the next departing guest by moving down the counter to rearrange some papers.

Shortly, I heard Leticia saying, "Is there anything else I can do for you?" Noticing that I had not left the counter, yet knowing there were others who deserved her attention, she could have ignored me on the basis that I was no longer a guest—but she didn't.

These three encounters exemplify the level of customer service every business would like to achieve. The secret lies in the way Leticia answered my question, “How long has this hotel been open?” “Less than two years,” she replied. “We’re young.” She could have said, “It’s young” or “They’re young”—but she didn’t. By including herself as a part of the hotel, she revealed the explanation for the considerate actions in all three encounters. It’s called “a sense of community,” and it only happens when a person acts as she would when she sees herself as part of something bigger than herself—whether that be a business, a church, a university, or a city—and it has universal application—from Waco to Istanbul.

A LESSON FROM LAMBARENE

He pursued his education to the point of receiving a doctorate in philosophy—but felt he should do more.

He pursued his education further, ultimately receiving the doctor of theology, doctor of music, and doctor of medicine degrees—but felt he should do more.

He pursued his interest in theology to the point of becoming principal of St. Thomas Theological College at the University of Strasbourg—but felt he should do more.

He pursued his interest in music to the point of giving numerous organ concerts each year, including annual engagements with the Paris Bach Society and the Orfeo Catalia in Spain—but felt he should do more.

He wrote books on theology including *The Quest*

for the Historical Jesus and *Christianity and the Religious World*—but felt he should do more.

He became an authority on the life and music of Johann Sebastian Bach and an interpreter of Bach's works—but felt he should do more.

He wrote a two-volume work, *The Philosophy of Civilization*, as well as other books including *Out of My Life and Thought*—and still felt he should do more.

He took the money from his organ concerts and his book royalties and went to the obscure African village of Lambarene and built a hospital.

And, when awarded the Nobel Peace Prize, he used the $33,000 from that award to expand the hospital and set up a leper colony.

His name was Albert Schweitzer.

When Norman Cousins went to Lambarene to visit this extraordinary man, he summarized his impressions in the following way: "The greatness of

Schweitzer—indeed the essence of Schweitzer—is the man as symbol. It is not so much what he has done for others, but what others have done because of him and the power of his example. This is the measure of the man. What has come out of his life and thought is the kind of inspiration that can animate a generation…Schweitzer's aim was not to dazzle an age but to awaken it, to make it comprehend that moral splendor is part of the gift of life…."

"Anyone that proposes to do good," Schweitzer wrote, "must not expect people to roll stones out of his way, but must accept his lot calmly if they ever roll a few more upon it."

In his own writings, Schweitzer describes the time he was able to label his motivation. While making a long, slow journey down an African river, feeling for the channel between the sandbanks, he was lost in thought as he sat on the deck of the barge; "at the very moment when, at sunset, we were making our way through the herd of hippopotamuses, there flashed upon my mind, unforeseen and un-thought, the phrase "Ehrfurcht vor dem leben." This German phrase means "reverence for life."

"Reverence for life," Schweitzer wrote, "does not allow the scholar to live for his science alone, even if he is very useful to the community in so doing. It does not permit the artist to exist only for his art, even if he gives inspiration to many by its means. It refuses to let the businessman imagine that he fulfills all legitimate demands in the course of his business activities."

Albert Schweitzer was deeply motivated by a spirit of genuine thanksgiving, or perhaps better stated as thanks — giving.

"In gratitude for your own good fortune," he wrote, "you must render in return some sacrifice of your life for other life."

Section I: Essential Expectations

Why do people move to cities? In 1800, only about 3% of the world's population lived in urban areas. Two hundred years later, the estimate has reached 50%.

As more and more people move to the cities, it should be helpful to understand their motivation. After listening to citizens, looking at surveys, and talking with local elected officials, I have identified five essential expectations that have sustained across the ages.

1. Safety. The need to find refuge has been, throughout history, a reason for people to come together. The early cities fortified themselves with heavy walls. For hundreds of years, the wall was one of the most universal symbols of a city. Today, the threat to safety has moved inside the city. But the expectation continues to exist that the city, through trained police, fire, and emergency response forces, will provide a different kind of protective wall.

Programs such as neighborhood policing and Neighborhood Watch represent attempts to implement a community dimension as part of the solution.

2. Health. In the early settlements, the availability of a reliable source of water was a prime concern. The importance of health has expanded today, especially as we see older families moving to the city from remote or rural locations specifically to be closer to the doctor or to medical facilities. Recreation facilities and fitness centers have added another dimension to the "quality of life" perspective of the expectations that fall in the general category of health. Also, the ability to find competent professional help in the areas of mental and emotional health is a growing concern.

3. Exchange. Perhaps the most obvious reason that people move from rural to urban life is to find work, to exchange a day's labor for a day's pay. The opportunity for cities to provide an area for people to come together at the marketplace for buying and selling has always been a major factor in the life of the city. The economic development component of the city is the contemporary acknowledgement that exchange is, indeed, an essential expectation.

4. Learning. The schoolhouse was one of the central buildings in even the smallest settlements of the American West. There was a time when the most learning opportunities were for the children and in the schoolhouse; today's challenge is to find ways to provide lifelong learning and training opportunities for all citizens. Learning means more than schoolroom education; learning can be accomplished in many places including libraries, museums, art galleries, concert halls, and zoos. In the 21st century's Information

Age, the expansive opportunities for learning for all the members of the family have never held greater importance.

5. Connectedness. If the first four elements seem to be more "city" than "community," I would suggest the reverse is true of connectedness. Edward Hallowell described connectedness in the following way: "It is a sense of being a part of something larger than oneself...It is a sense of accompaniment. It is that feeling in your bones that you are not alone. It is a sense that no matter how scary things may become, there is a hand for you in the dark. While ambition drives us to achieve, connectedness is my word for the force that urges us to ally, to affiliate, to enter into mutual relationships, to take strength and to grow through cooperative behavior."

The ways that people find to develop a sense of belonging in the places where they live is extremely important. In Anton Chekhov's classic play, *Three*

Sisters, Andrei says "You can go to an enormous restaurant in Moscow, you may not know anyone, no one knows you, you still have the feeling you belong." That's the universal hope, the essential expectation for the cities, large or small, in which we live.

Edmund Burke wrote about how connectedness or being "attached" begins. "To be attached to the subdivision, to love the little platoon we belong to in society, is the first principle (the germ as it were) of public affections."

These, I believe, are the five essential expectations—Safety, Health, Exchange, Learning, and Connectedness. As mentioned in the introduction, to the extent that the "city" can deliver the tangible components and the "community" can deliver the intangible part of each of the five, the people will not only come but will most likely stay. More will be said about the ways "community" plays a part in all five expectations in the reflections which follow.

LIFE IS DANGEROUS...

"Harken to me now, ye men of Ithaca, to the word that I shall say."

With these words an old man stood in the midst of other men and began to speak. In his epic poem, *The Odyssey*, the ancient Greek Homer described the older man with the following words, "Then in the midst up rose Mentor, the companion of noble Odysseus. He it was to whom Odysseus, as he departed in the fleet, had given the charge over all his house, that it should obey the old man, and that he should keep all things safe."

The *Odyssey* was written around 800 B.C., but over 2,700 years later, the process of asking someone to accept the responsibility to "keep all things safe" has continued. Safety is an essential expectation of community.

The earliest ideas of the city must have developed with the idea of enhancing safety. Lewis Mumford reports that as early as 913, there were reports that "the building of fortresses and of walls around settlements was one of the chief activities of the King's army." The famous fall of the walls of the city of Jericho (perhaps the oldest continuously occupied city in the world) dates back to 1250 B.C. The rose-red "city of rock," Petra, Jordan, the capital city of the Nabataean empire, provided a naturally walled and practically impenetrable enclosure for its occupants from the fifth century B.C. to the fifth century A.D.

According to Mumford, the idea of a moat and walls *keeping all things safe* was effective until the fifteenth century. About that time, "new artillery made cities vulnerable" and their old form of defense "just made them more conspicuous targets."

Much has changed in our cities since the days of Petra, Jericho, and Ithaca; yet surveys of contemporary society continue to indicate that keeping "all things safe" remains an essential expectation. Neighborhood policing and watch programs represent some of the recent attempts to enhance the degree of community safety.

On April 19, 1995 cities everywhere were shockingly introduced into a new era of vulnerability. It happened in Oklahoma City at 9:03 a.m.—terror struck the heartland of America—and 168 men, women and children lost their lives.

City leaders everywhere were reminded of their Mentor-like responsibility to "keep all things safe" and how each member of the community must share in that responsibility if we are truly to enjoy the opportunities for life, liberty, and the pursuit of happiness.

The responsibility we share for each other's safety was refreshingly and succinctly captured in a billboard message. Having just landed in Sydney, Australia and taking the cab into town, I was confronted by a single six-word message: "Life is dangerous. Learn first aid."

Roseto: The Second Discovery

In the 1790s in the town of Rosetta, Egypt, a curious discovery was made. A stone was found by a French expedition. The message recorded on the stone was only partially decipherable. A young man named Jean-Francois Champollion eventually studied the message text. Champollion, fluent in Arabic, Calidonian, Syrian, and Coptic languages, determined that the stone actually contained a single message copied in three languages—Greek, Egyptian Demotic, and hieroglyphics. By comparing the known language to the unknown, Champollion was able to break the code to the then undecipherable hieroglyphic language of ancient Egypt, thus making it possible to read hundreds of writings on ancient tombs and temples.

More than a century and a half later, in the 1960s in a town with the similar sounding name of Roseto, Pennsylvania, another curious discovery was made.

Research indicated that the people of Roseto were healthier than those of surrounding towns; in fact they were among the healthiest in the United States. Roseto looked much like many other small towns in the wooded mountains of eastern Pennsylvania; the people of Roseto didn't seem to exercise more; their risk factors for heart disease such as smoking and high-fat diets seemed no different.

But there was an important difference. Dr. Stewart Wolf, a professor at the University of Oklahoma School of Medicine, isolated that difference. Roseto had been settled in 1882 by immigrants from southern Italy. Dr. Wolf found that the tight-knit community of mutual support and cohesiveness "served to counteract the effects of life stress and thereby were a protective against heart disease." Involvement in their neighborhood, in civic and community organizations, and in their church were all positive factors.

But things have begun to change in Roseto.

According to Mark Harris, "The younger generation increasingly took work outside of the region, church attendance slipped, and the number of three-generational households declined." Modern-day Roseto began to see more fences and satellite dishes. Then in 1971, the first heart attack of anyone under 45 was recorded. Sadly, by the year 2000, Roseto's rates of heart disease and longevity matched the national average. In his book *Love and Survival*, Dr. Dean Ornish documents several other studies that reach similar conclusions. Ornish summarizes the consistent pattern of these studies by observing that "Those who were socially isolated had at least two to five times the risk of premature death from all causes when compared to those who had a strong sense of connection and community."

Dr. Wolf had a name for it. He referred to the health benefit of living in a strong community as "the Roseto Effect."

PART OF THE TOWN

His name is Vedran Smailovic.

I've never met him. But his story, as reported by the *New York Times* in June 1992, has left a deep personal impression.

Some might have considered his behavior a bit strange.

Each afternoon at four o'clock, Mr. Smailovic, dressed in formal evening attire, unfolded a plastic chair in the middle of Vase Miskina Street, took his cello from its case, and began playing Albinoni's *Adagio*.

Even though Vase Miskina Street was located near a pedestrian mall, there was no audience. But Mr. Smailovic was not playing for applause.

Mr. Smailovic is a citizen of Sarajevo.

His city, once known around the world as the picturesque host of the 1984 Winter Olympics, was being torn apart by civil war.

As a boy, he grew up in this narrow valley surrounded by the breathtaking natural grandeur of spectacular seasonal changes in the mountains.

Now he was witnessing a different spectacle, the eerie sights and sounds of flares and gunfire—the antithesis of community.

It was a difficult time for the citizens of Sarajevo, a city nestled in the high mountains of Bosnia and Herzegovina. Their hometown, which managed to survive two world wars with only minor damage, was being terrorized. The *Times* report described Sarajevo as "a wasteland of blasted mosques, churches and museums, of fire-gutted office towers, hotels and sports stadiums and of hospitals, music schools and libraries punctured by rockets, mortars and artillery shells."

Despair was high in Sarajevo. Some would flee.

Some would complain. Some would wring their hands.

But not Vedran Smailovic. He had to respond. He had to do something.

The site of his daily concert was chosen for a specific reason. At this location, many of his fellow citizens were standing in a bread line outside a bakery on May 27, 1992 when several high explosive rounds suddenly hit the crowded area. More than one hundred people were wounded; 22 were killed.

According to his plan, Mr. Smailovic would perform Albinoni's *Adagio* each day for 22 days. It was his personal way of honoring his 22 fellow citizens who lost their lives.

Through his actions, Mr. Smailovic provides a universal insight about the relationship that exists between an individual and his community. This 36-year-old man, who played cello for the Sarajevo opera, explained in simple yet eloquent terms the key to "community."

"I am nothing special," he said. "I am a musician. I am part of the town. Like everyone else, I do what I can."

His name is Vedran Smailovic—proud, caring citizen of Sarajevo.

May his tribe increase in cities throughout the world.

THE STATISTICAL WELL-BEING OF BRIDGES

What is the ultimate compliment that can be given to a city? Perhaps it was given to Amsterdam: "More than any other major city in Europe, Amsterdam seems to have been designed with people in mind." Later in the same section from Birnbaum's travel guide, the following somewhat surprising statement is made: "Amsterdam has more canals than Venice...spanned by some 1,000 bridges" (Venice has 400).

Is it merely a coincidence that the city of 1,000 bridges just happens to be considered the best designed with people in mind?

While sitting in a waiting room, I picked up a September 1996 issue of *Smithsonian* magazine. Flipping through the pages, an article on bridges in America caught my attention:

"Today there are some 600,000 public bridges in

the United States, of which almost 35 percent are in need of repair or replacement. After a long period of neglect, we are now entering a new era of bridge building and repairing."

On the surface, the statistical well-being of America's bridges makes very little difference to most of us. Few of us feel involved in the bridge-building business.

But there is another sense in which the building and repairing of bridges is of great importance to every community, every business, every church, every family, and every person. These are the more important, unseen, uncountable bridges that connect people to people.

In his book *Future Shock*, Alvin Toffler wrote of the value of long duration relationships, sometimes called friendships, which are the result of the unseen bridges.

He suggested the long-lasting relationships in our lives are becoming as rare as "long-stemmed flowers towering above a field of grass in which each blade represents a short-term relationship."

Toffler observed it is the very duration of these ties that makes them noticeable.

Visible bridges are built with concrete, steel, asphalt, gravel, and rock.

Unseen bridges are built with trust, respect, compassion, encouragement, and love. Both need continuous attention.

Unseen bridges are as essential to community as visible bridges are to the city.

Both will deteriorate from inattention and neglect. Each can be shaken and damaged by the literal or figurative crises of flood waters, excessive heat or cold, undue or unanticipated stress, and earthquakes.

The 600,000 visible bridges in the United States make it possible to travel easily throughout the nation. Similarly, regarding community, we all live in Amsterdam, where thousands of unseen bridges are essential for people to deal better with the difficult times in their lives and to have a sense of connectedness.

It is reassuring to know "after a long period of neglect, we are now entering a new era" of building and repairing our public bridges.

It is more essential than ever that each of us determine to launch a new era of daily building and repairing the unseen bridges. There are many ways to build and maintain these unseen bridges in our lives. But one basic rule always seems to prevail with regard to effective bridge building. For 2,000 years, it has been passed from one generation to another.

Knowing his death was near, former tennis great Arthur Ashe passed along this essential rule for building unseen bridges in a farewell letter to his daughter. He wrote these words, "Be ruled by that rule called golden."

BIRTHDAY NUMBER 101

July 7, 2001—George Dawson died two days ago. I didn't know him. I never met him. But I wish I had.

I read his newspaper obituary in the Abilene paper. The heading read "Man who inspired others by learning to read at 98 dies at 103." The story told of this grandson of a slave, George Dawson, born on January 18, 1898 in Marshall, Texas. He had started working at age 12 for $1.50 a month. He had never stopped working long enough to go to school. His jobs had included driving spikes for the railroad, working in a sawmill, breaking horses in the Texas Panhandle, and after he married and settled in Dallas, where he also died, working for a dairy. He and his wife had seven children; all went to college.

But George Dawson had never learned to read—until he was 98. According to the obituary,

"Dawson said the turning point of his life came the day a literacy volunteer knocked on his door and asked if he'd like to learn to read."

In Dawson's memoirs, titled *Life is So Good*, co-authored by elementary school teacher Richard Glaubman, his "first day of school was January 4, 1996," when he was ninety-eight years old. He said the best part of his ninety-ninth birthday was being able to read the birthday cards—"I couldn't do that for the first ninety-eight birthdays."

As George Dawson attended classes at the Lincoln Instructional Center in Dallas, his instructor reported that he inspired others, that "his work ethic and commitment" helped the younger students.

Dawson stated, "Ever since I turned a hundred...life has been busy. After school, lots of days I'll go visiting. Mostly to schools and talk to children." He received so many calls that he was advised to limit his trips. Dawson responded, "But there's a lot of people that need some help."

To mark birthday number 101, so many wanted to celebrate with Dawson that a hall was rented at the community center. Months after his birthday, he was still receiving cards—and reading them.

"I never thought I was too old to learn," the one hundred and three-year-old Dawson said. He was right, but he also never grew too old to inspire others. Perhaps "learning" and "helping others" should always fit together, and should be two things from which we never retire.

The Humble Collection

The collection of B.J. Humble is no ordinary collection. While many were collecting butterflies, stamps or coins, Humble was collecting lamps.

But these are not ordinary lamps—none electric, nor even kerosene. Over a period of twenty years, which included fifteen trips to the Holy Land, Humble has collected more than 72 lamps that date from 2,000 B.C. to 700 A.D.

These durable clay containers were designed to hold a wick in olive oil. Over the years, the shapes and markings of the oil lamps changed; lamps thus have become one of archaeology's most important sources for dating time periods.

As I viewed the Humble collection, one particular lamp caught my attention. Its shape was distinctly Roman—round, with a short spout. After spending more than 1,500 years in the waters of the

Mediterranean Sea near Gaza, this lamp was discovered in amazingly excellent condition. The top was covered with artwork from a trained hand; a man, perhaps Apollo, is portrayed fighting a large snake.

However, I had not yet seen its most striking single element. Turning this small clay artifact over to reveal the base, I was suddenly confronted with an unspoken explanation for the quality of this ancient artwork—the mark of the craftsman!

There, in clear relief, was a remarkable reminder of the enduring relationship that can exist between the worker and his work.

It is a relationship reserved for people with the attitude of a craftsman—people who see their work as something more than merely a means for making money, people who establish the highest quality standards for themselves, people who are willing to place their own distinctive personal mark on their work.

Perhaps it was easier to sign one's work during the age of the craftsman, when practically everything was made by hand. In an era that seems to be earning the labels of "The Post Industrial Society" or "The Information Age," many work at jobs that provide a service rather than a product. But the fact that we do not always have a tangible product upon which to leave our personal mark should not become an excuse for allowing excellence to be displaced by mediocrity.

The key does not lie in whether one has a product upon which to place his mark. The key is whether one approaches one's work with the same attitude of the ancient oil lamp craftsman who knew that his signed work became a reflection of the worker.

On a road trip through Tennessee, my wife and I left the interstate for the beautiful countryside. Saturday morning found us in the recently restored central business district of Columbia. While I walked around the courthouse square, Sylvia stepped into one of the nicely renovated old storefronts. I returned to find "we" had made several purchases, involving extended visits with an engaging proprietor named Carolyn. We left with some unique gifts of art and positive impressions from our first and only visit to Columbia. We had met only one person, but fortunately for both us and her community, a person who honored the spirit of craftsmanship. As we were leaving her store she gave us one thing more—her business card—which contained three names, all benefiting from the quality of her work: her name, the name of her business, and the name of her city.

A true craftsman does not seek the veil of anonymity in order to hide from being accountable for defective products or shoddy service. A craftswoman realizes her personal reputation, the reputation of her organization, and the reputation of her community can be enhanced or diminished by the quality of her work.

The people who wish to honor the tradition of true craftsmanship know that, even when it may seem impossible to actually do so, they are always willing to sign their work.

A Brief Business Exchange

Ralph Waldo Emerson wrote about the importance of enjoying our work:

"The crowning fortune of a man is to be born to some pursuit which finds him employment and happiness, whether it is to make baskets, or broadswords, or canals, or statutes or songs."

Less eloquent, but more succinct, was the sign I noticed while visiting in one businessman's office: "The first step to success is to like what you're doing."

Not long ago I stopped in an Abilene camera store, not planning to make any purchases, but simply to sample the equipment and check the prices. Because of an upcoming trip, I was considering the possibility of a new lens.

A salesclerk named JoAnn promptly came to the counter and asked if she could help. I gave her the shopper's traditional response: "No, thank you. I'm just looking."

But the reply did not have its usual effect. JoAnn didn't walk away. I'm still unable to explain why I was soon telling her about the camera and lens I was presently using, and about the kinds of pictures I hoped to take on the forthcoming trip.

About 30 minutes later, I left the store with a new lens, two filters, a cleaning kit, a flash attachment, and six rolls of film.

As I was leaving, the owner of the camera shop was entering. We visited briefly and I told him about the purchases I had made and the pleasant salesclerk. He supplied some background information. JoAnn had been hired to work in the darkroom and had done so for several years. Growing weary of that work, she asked for a chance to work in sales. He gave her a chance; it proved to be the right decision: "She's one of the best we've ever had," he said.

Over a lifetime, we make many purchases and meet many salesclerks. Most of these brief business exchanges are quickly forgotten. Occasionally, however, we encounter someone who transforms the mundane into the memorable.

I think I know why JoAnn was so effective in her job. She subscribes to a slightly contrarian school of thought that believes "work is more fun than fun."

I know this is true because as she closed the sale and handed me the package, she didn't say the traditional "Thank you" or "Come back again." She said something that I've never heard a salesclerk say before or since.

She said, "It's been fun."

Section II: Existing Elements

❖

While the first section focused on essential expectations, this section deals with five existing elements that strongly influence the individuality of the city and ceaselessly shape its identity. These are the "five cards" that each city has been dealt. They are unique to each city—no other city in the world has exactly these same "cards." They cannot be discarded or ignored—in fact, the more fully we are aware of them, understand them, and interpret them in terms of their contemporary meaning and potential impact, the clearer should be the plans and goals for the city.

The five existing elements are: Geography, History, Demographics, Heritage, and Culture.

1. Geography. The dramatic variances of terrain in Toledo are powerfully portrayed in El Greco's painting *View of Toledo.* The city of Toledo is located south of Madrid in Spain. It is primarily a farming and ranching town surrounded by vineyards and fields of wheat, cotton, and tobacco. The city, perched upon a hill, overlooks the River Tagus and the Montes de Toledo (Toledo Mountains), which rise majestically in the background. The climate varies from hot summers to cold winters, from much sunshine to little rain. One cannot deny that Toledo is indeed a unique city when seen through the eyes of El Greco. Its geography, or specifically the natural features of that region, determines many of these attributes of the city of Toledo that make it a distinctive place.

In the same way, every city in the world, large and small, is largely defined by its geographic position. It is clear that "a city's location is the first key to its form, structure and history."

2. History. There is an old Latin proverb that says "History is the mother of life." A more generally used definition is that history is the record of the past events of a place or a people; more simply, history is the stories that are passed down throughout the generations. These stories communicate identity. These stories shape who we are as a community. The collective stories of a community which are remembered and retold shape *who* that community *is*. Essentially, as Emerson observed, "The city…lives by remembering."

The Great Chicago Fire on October 8, 1871 forever changed the identity of that city. One hundred thousand Chicagoans lost their homes; eighteen thousand buildings were burned; and around two hundred million dollars of property was destroyed on that day. The fire not only changed the face of the city, but it also changed the attitudes of its citizens. The locals were resilient, unwilling to be daunted by this disaster. As one prominent citizen observed: "Chicago is not burnt up, only well blistered for bad ailments, to strengthen her for manhood." That single event is unique to the history of Chicago; essentially, it factored in shaping the city and its citizens.

Rotterdam experienced a similarly dramatic change in its story when, during World War II, the German army used its blitzkrieg strategy to destroy the heart of the city. Devastating though it was, they had no choice but to rebuild almost completely the city center from scratch. Today Rotterdam has one of the finest ports in the world.

The history of a city is a long, continuing story. Each story has its prologue (or events leading up to its birth), an introduction (or the beginnings of its settlement and building of its infrastructure), and chapters (which are still being written with each passing year). Those stories can serve to unite the citizens of a place in a sense of community—as poet laureate Robert Pinsky said, "A people is defined and unified not by blood but by shared memory."

3. Demographics. The statistical characteristics of a population comprise another existing element in the make-up of a city. The number of people or the ethnic mix of people in a city can be an important determinant of identity. Juneau, Alaska has very interesting demographics. With fewer than 50,000 citizens, 29.3% are under 18 years, and only 5.1% are over 65; additionally, 12.9% of its citizens are Alaskan Natives. As far as education is concerned, 89.9% of its citizens are high school graduates, and 30.7% have a college degree. In 1990, the number of adults not in the workforce was 25% of the population, with an unemployment rate of 4.8%. The median household income was $47,924; 5.5% of the citizens were living below the poverty level.

Another aspect of its demographic statistics that separates Juneau from other cities is the fact that its city limits encompass the largest landmass of any city in the United States—larger than the state of Delaware! Part of this area includes glaciers and ice fields that cannot be developed. I doubt that any other city has as much space per citizen as Juneau—or the same demographic profile.

The demographics of cities are constantly changing. Since demographic data cannot be controlled, it must be monitored. It tells us much about the changing face of the city and the implied opportunities or problems that should be anticipated.

4. Heritage. The city of Delft, Holland has a rich heritage, or legacy of what is passed down from its predecessors. It began in the 1600s when China, the primary supplier throughout the world of a unique design of blue and white porcelain that had become very popular, was experiencing brutal civil wars. However, with the onset of the civil wars, China was unable to produce enough porcelain to supply the demand at that time. Potters in Delft saw their opportunity; immediately artisans began to design and sell their own version of the pottery. Thus, Delftware was born, and has since become the trademark of the small town. The heritage that was passed down was more than a pottery design; it was a value system that included quality craftsmanship.

Heritage is the legacy of values that descends from one's predecessors. Each generation would do well to be sure that the best lessons learned from the previous generation are passed along. In this way, the torch is passed, and light is provided for the journey into the uncertain future.

5. Culture. Culture is an accumulation of the deeply rooted beliefs, habits, customs, and traditions of the people in a place. In a time when deeply rooted beliefs are hard to come by and the search for self-discovery has become a popular pastime with ever-changing results, culture is struggling for a foothold in society. Still, every city should work to maintain the unique flavor it has gradually developed over time. In each city and town, there should be an ongoing program of cultural excavation and discovery.

Salzburg, Austria was the birthplace of Wolfgang Mozart, and his legacy has been woven into the fabric of the city so that it has forever shaped its cultural heritage. With annual year-round festivals and celebrations, Salzburg commemorates its most famous son in many ways, including the grand Salzburg Festival, which lasts almost a month and a half each summer.

Through cultural activities such as those Salzburg incorporates into its regular schedule of events, citizen involvement increases. In fact, John Kreidler suggests "cities with high cultural involvement from the community result in having excellent schools and universities, fine public health programs, and virtually no juvenile delinquency." Culture must be a key in the development of strong communities.

THE SISTERHOOD OF CITIES

In the 1990s, the city of Abilene and the city of Corinth, Greece entered into a joint agreement to be Sister Cities. Perhaps the first result of such agreements is a raised awareness—each becomes more aware of the other, perhaps especially in the ways we are different—different languages, different currency, different foods, and different customs.

Different Ages: The site known as Corinth has been inhabited for more than seven thousand years—Abilene was founded in 1881—only slightly more than one hundred years ago.

Different Histories: Following the Corinthian War (395-387 B.C.), Corinth began to gather strength and became the largest and most important city in Greece from 350 B.C. through 250 B.C. After a period of decline, the city flourished again and foreigners, especially Italians and Jews, came to settle there between 50 B.C. and 60 A.D. It was during this time that the Apostle Paul visited and wrote his well-known letters to the Corinthians.

Over the ensuing years Corinth endured earthquakes, fires, and floods; today, seven pillars from the ancient temple of Apollo stand surrounded by other ruins of the past, while the new city of Corinth has been built along the sea something less than five miles away.

As I read through the Kaloyeropoulou account of the history of Corinth, the dissimilarities with Abilene were strikingly apparent and abundant. But there was one short paragraph in which I found an underlying principle for understanding the reason all cities are different, a sense in which all cities share a universal sisterhood: "No one has yet fully discovered what are the fundamental causes that have led a people to flourish or decline, or exactly what conditions dictate its destiny. Nevertheless, even if we accept the existence of imponderable factors, one thing about Corinth is certain: Its geographic position played an enormously important role in its development...But, after saying this, we should not omit to mention how greatly the successive inhabitants of this site exploited the unique advantages."

Geographic position also played a part in the development of Abilene. In 1881, when the tracks were being laid westward for the Texas and Pacific line, the railroad needed a stop in West Texas at a point that was first designated as Milepost 407. On March 15 an auction was held, and 187 lots were purchased along each side of the railroad tracks; thus the city of Abilene was born.

As with every city, our geographic position has been the reason for much that has happened since—both good (industries such as ranching and oil) and bad (weather including tornadoes and droughts).

Therein lies both the opportunity and the challenge—the "successive inhabitants" must continue to understand the nuances of geographic position and to "exploit the unique advantages" that may occur over time.

All advantages are not entirely obvious—for years San Antonio viewed its river as a nuisance, even a liability; yet today the "River Walk" is truly a "unique advantage." Occasionally, geographic positioning can even originate as a negative that ultimately becomes an unanticipated positive.

When the devastating floods and fires struck Grand Forks, North Dakota, no one could at first see a silver living. But 20,000 volunteers came to lend their help; churches, charities, and corporations worked together as never before; citizens looked beyond their own needs to help neighbors who were "worse off."

"We are not the same people we were last year," said Mayor Pat Owens. "But we're better, because we've learned what we need to value. We've learned what matters."

Geographic position provides each place not only with obvious and unique advantages but also, at times, with some not-so-obvious benefits—if we are just perceptive enough to see them.

TESTIMONY TO THE PASSING OF TIME

It was a cold December evening as I rushed along the snowy Philadelphia sidewalks. My meetings had concluded only minutes before closing time; it was almost dark when the guards let the last few visitors into the old Pennsylvania State House and then locked the door. As I joined the day's last group, the guide had already begun his lecture and the crowd was pressed against the banister. Only half listening, I tried to move inconspicuously through the back of the group, the object of my search yet unseen. Edging to the side I gained a better vantage-point and there it was.

Early in the Constitutional Convention, George Washington had been selected to serve as chairman. Each day he sat in the same chair, this very same chair, at the front of this room. Reports indicate that he actually said comparatively little, but his presence was extremely important, if for no other reason than because of the dignity and distinction he lent to the occasion. Now as his work neared completion, each man began to affix his signature to the document that shaped the American democracy.

Only then did Benjamin Franklin disclose that throughout the convention, he had continued to study the decorative carving of a radiant sun on the horizon at the top of Washington's chair.

On September 17, 1787, as the work of the Philadelphia convention was nearing completion, Franklin had finally come to a conclusion about the sun: "I have the happiness to know," he then observed, "it is a rising sun and not a setting sun."

Over two hundred years after Franklin's historic "proclamation," it is interesting to note that only two artifacts remain from the original furnishings of the Constitutional Convention meeting room—an inkwell and George Washington's chair.

More than an artifact of a great moment in history, the chair with the "rising sun" is an enduring symbol of the optimistic leadership so necessary to the life of a nation, a state, or a city.

Conclusion Number One: History Illuminates Reality

The house looked very much like all the other houses along the sidewalk, which looked very much like all the other sidewalks in the neighborhood—rather unremarkable. It would have been easy to miss except for the gathering at the front steps of a small group of people—many of them young—most of them girls.

But it was not just any street; it was Prinsengracht. It was not just any house; it was a house where a young girl once lived. And she was not just any girl; she was a remarkable fourteen-year-old girl named Anne Frank.

According to the guidebook, "A short way west

of the Dam and just around the corner from the Westerkerk is the house containing the secret annex where the Frank family and their friends hid from the Nazis for two years. No matter how prepared you are, you will be shocked by the size and vulnerability of the quarters that housed Anne, her parents, their friends the Van Daans, their teenaged son Peter and a dentist named Dussel. You'll go in behind a bookcase that disguised the entrance to the upstairs hideout and see the simple artifacts, photos and newspaper clippings that speak so mutely and eloquently of tragic times."

But what the guidebook does not, and probably cannot accurately describe, is the hushed, self-imposed silence with which this procession of visitors from all over the world slowly, very slowly, moves through the rooms—and the quiet tears that slowly, very slowly, move down the cheeks of the young and old—many of whom remember reading that unforgettable diary in their own language; but now they respond in the universal language of the heart.

Conclusion Number Two: History Vitalizes Memory

"Some think I do wrong to go to the opera and the theatre; but it rests me," Abraham Lincoln once admitted. "I love to be alone and yet with people. I want to get this burden off, to change the current of my thoughts. A hearty laugh relieves me; and I seem better able after it to bear my cross."

He had attended Ford's Theatre nine times prior to the evening of April 14, 1865. On that evening he went to enjoy a performance of *Our American Cousin*, starring Laura Keene. But the evening was shattered by the bullet of assassin John Wilkes Booth.

Following that tragic night, Ford's Theatre was closed. For over 100 years the stage remained dark, until February 12, 1968 when Ford's Theatre was reopened following three years of careful reconstruction based on the photographs of Civil War photographer Matthew Brady.

As if stepping 122 years back into history, I purchased a Ford's Theatre balcony ticket to attend Arthur Miller's play *All My Sons*, starring Richard Kiley.

Some interesting parallels began to emerge during that evening in Ford's Theatre. Abraham Lincoln had struggled under the weight of a country torn by slavery. Arthur Miller's play was set in the post-World War II era and focused on a country torn by war. Now, Richard Kiley was presenting a World War II story from a Civil War platform, melding a common message of man dealing with the churning upheavals of life.

As I looked across the balcony to that dark and always empty box in Ford's Theatre, I thought that its one-time occupant would have appreciated the timelessness of this message about man's moral responsibilities.

Leaving the theatre, I paused in front of the narrow four-story red brick building across the street. A small simple plaque had been affixed to the outside wall: "Abraham Lincoln died in this house April 15, 1865 at 7:22 a.m."

Less than two months prior to this date, Lincoln had delivered his second inaugural address; it was characteristically brief. But it contained an insight into the wisdom of one who had lived life fully aware of his moral responsibilities.

On this night the words had fresh meaning: "With malice toward none; with charity for all; with firmness in the right, as God gives us to see the right, let us strive on to finish the work we are in...."

Conclusion Three: History Provides Guidance in Daily Life

On a warm April day in the year 2000, with carefully numbered steps, I found myself surrounded in an eerie aura of antiquity that dated back more than one thousand, five hundred years. In those ninety-one carefully counted steps, I had gained a remarkable perspective of the best-known Mayan ruin, located on the Yucatan peninsula. The ancient city of Chechen Itza has gone through several cycles, from heavy population to complete desolation, from the most important city in Yucatan to an abandoned ghost town. Today it joins other ancient cities such as Petra, Jordan and Ephesus, Turkey; about all three, it is said that only a fraction of the city has thus far been excavated.

Those ninety-one steps led to the top of the majestically powerful four-sided pyramid known as "El Castillo," which continues to honor the amazing architectural genius and astronomical acumen of an enigmatic people of long ago. As night fell, it shrouded most visible reminders of the modern era;

in the darkness a moving sound-and-light show completed the journey into a once-great city populated by some of the earliest inhabitants of our Americas. Stories were told of the high-stakes games played on the ball court, the fascinating murals from the temple of warriors, a mysterious stone jaguar imbedded with large pieces of jade, and a curious underground river which fed the Sacred well.

Conclusion Number Four: History Brings Us Tidings of Antiquity

These four points are not original with me, but what if Washington's chair had been discarded, what if the Frank's house had been destroyed, what if Ford's Theatre had been razed long ago, and what if the stones of Chechen Itza had been scattered? They each serve to remind us that Cicero was correct when over two thousand years ago he wrote:

> History is the witness
> that testifies to the passing of time;

it illumines reality,
vitalizes memory,
provides guidance in daily life
and brings us tidings of antiquity.

But preservation of our history is not only important for chairs in Philadelphia, houses in Amsterdam, theaters in Washington, D.C., and cities like Chechen Itza. It is important in your city and in mine. Perhaps we can respectfully reinforce Cicero's thoughts with a few additional observations.

I am so grateful for some far-sighted people in my city of Abilene who, several years ago, decided that the old Paramount Theatre should be carefully and completely restored as a venue for classic movies and live performances. So often it is the restoration of public places such as theaters that reattaches us in important ways.

Conclusion Number Five: Historic Preservation

Connects and Reconnects People to Places and People to People.

Just outside Abilene, to the north, rock chimneys stand as silent sentries continuing to guard the scattered vestiges of a brief but important time in the settling of the American West. The place is called Fort Phantom. The story goes that from a distance, the approaching riders looked across the steamy, flat, summer horizon of West Texas to view the strange sight of a fort seeming to float as a ghost hovers above the ground.

Today, the recently formed, multi-faceted alliance to advance a cooperative effort called Texas Fort Trails represents good news. All the Texas Travel Trails will benefit the entire state of Texas at a time when travel and tourism is the largest and fastest-growing industry in the world.

Conclusion Number Six: Historic Preservation Attracts—and is often the most effective way to

create a local industry of destination tourism.

In Abilene, the railroad runs right through the middle of our town, and right through the middle of our identity. Slightly more than ten years ago, the depot and the three other buildings directly connected with our 119-year railroad history were on the brink of extinction. Thankfully the depot is now completely restored and serves as the visitor center and office of the cultural affairs council. The other buildings now house museums and a chocolate candy maker.

In a world filled with parking lots and temporary buildings, it is nice to be reminded that some things last, and that there are still some things worth keeping.

Conclusion Number Seven: Historic Preservation Authenticates and keeps us in touch with the reality of our heritage.

One May evening I walked through the streets of San Antonio and did what I always am drawn to do when I am in San Antonio—I visited the Alamo. There the stories come alive again—of Davy Crockett, Jim Bowie, and William Barrett Travis—of pride, determination, and courage.

There is only one Alamo. That piece of history which has been preserved so well and visited by so many makes this city different from every other city in the world.

Conclusion Number Eight: Historic Preservation Differentiates—and reminds us that in spite of all the fast food chain restaurants and all the shopping malls surrounded by asphalt, there are still ways each city and town is refreshingly unique.

In San Antonio some familiar words still seem to reverberate in the cool night air, more than a hollow echo from history. They are a reminder to each of us that it is important to Remember the Alamo—and all our Alamos, in all our cities.

The Prime Ingredient

While in Chicago I had the opportunity to enjoy one of the nice aspects about our American culture, the tasteful tradition of sharing a meal with good friends.

They had made reservations for Lawry's The Prime Rib, a restaurant with a fascinating history and a proven formula for success.

Lawrence L. Frank founded Lawry's The Prime Rib in Los Angeles in 1938 with his partner, Walter Van de Kamp. Their goal was to serve only one entrée and to make it "one of the greatest meals in America."

Most restaurants across the country have been involved in a non-stop process of modifying, diversifying, and expanding their menus, but for decades Lawry's The Prime Rib has continued to serve a tossed green salad (Salad Bowl à la Lawry's), baked potato, Yorkshire pudding, and prime rib with whipped-cream horseradish. To enhance the taste of the roast beef, Frank developed his own special seasoning that was so popular the customers took the bottles home with them, prompting the commercial birth of Lawry's Seasoned Salt.

For thirty-six years, there was only one Lawry's The Prime Rib. Then in 1974, after much debate, Lawrence Frank's son, Richard N. Frank, persuaded his father that the same distinctive character and quality could be duplicated in Chicago.

The chosen location was appropriately unique and distinctive. The 19th-century mansion at the corner of Rush and Ontario Streets was the former residence of L. Hamilton McCormick, inventor, writer, art collector and nephew of Cyrus Hall McCormick of reaping machine fame.

Good food and a pleasant atmosphere are essential ingredients in a recipe for success in the restaurant industry. But Lawry's The Prime Rib has included another less visible ingredient that permeates the entire organization, much like the effect of its seasoning salt on fine beef.

Just inside the entry of this impressive Chicago restaurant hangs an unpretentious plaque that yields insight into the secrets of long-term success. The plaque reads as follows:

Lawry's Code of Ethics

In the conduct of our business, we are and will continue to be guided by the following principles and ethics:

- We will be fair and truthful in our relations with our shareholders, our customers, our co-workers, our suppliers and with the public at large.
- We will be forthright and honest in all our dealings and relationships.
- We will be enlightened, aware of and

responsive to the changing world in which we reside.

- We will be responsible and exemplary citizens and constructive members of the various communities of which we are a part.
- We will constantly strive to improve upon all that we do.
- We will conduct our business in a manner which will enable us to take pride in our efforts and in the products and services which we provide.
- We will act in a manner which will earn the respect and esteem of all concerned.
- We regard as imperative the financial success, stability and growth of our business in consonance with these principles.

Hanging a code of ethics on the wall does not make the difference. The challenge is to take those principles off the plaque and bring them to life in the people of the organization.

In our skeptical society, it's easy to pass by an engraved plaque and remain unaffected. We are much more impressed by people than plaques. The Code of Ethics at Lawry's The Prime Rib came to life in a memorable way in the person of a "co-worker" named Genisse. At Lawry's there are no employees; everyone is a co-worker.

When I asked Genisse if she had enjoyed the six years of working at Lawry's, she responded with an enthusiastic, "Yes!"

Then I asked her, "Why?"

She quickly replied, "Because they treat you with respect."

It's probably not a coincidence that her words

and the seventh statement in Lawry's Code of Ethics seem strikingly similar.

There is something remarkable about those seven "we" statements of Lawry's. They seem to create a feeling of collective commitment that provides an insight into the essence of community. And they have a familiar ring with another set of "we" statements made by the people of an entire city:

> We will never bring disgrace to this our city by any act of dishonesty or cowardice, nor ever desert our suffering comrades in the ranks;
>
> We will fight for the ideal and sacred things of the city, both alone and with many;
>
> We will revere and obey the city's laws and do our best to incite a like respect in those above us who are prone to annul or set them at naught;

We will strive unceasingly to quicken the
public's sense of civic duty.
Thus, in all these ways,
We will transmit this city greater and more
beautiful than it was transmitted to us.

It was called "The Athenian Oath." In fourth century B.C., the young men of Athens took the oath when they reached the age of seventeen. There is a certain golden, ageless quality about coming together to "fight for the ideal."

WHAT PEOPLE NEED TO HEAR

On July 17, 1992 in an emotional, televised address to his nation, Vaclav Havel announced his plans to resign as president of Czechoslovakia. Negotiations between the Czechs and the Slovaks had become deadlocked, and his country seemed irretrievably destined for division.

It was a heartbreaking day for Havel, a former playwright who was so outspoken against Communism that he was labeled a dissident and imprisoned in 1979 for three years.

My thoughts rapidly went back two and a half years to another memorable event on January 1, 1990. Forty years of Communist rule had ended. As the new president Havel made his first major speech, he personified the people's dream of the dawning of a new era. The impact of Havel's speech was compared to Abraham Lincoln's previously mentioned second inaugural address.

Time magazine reported, "As an inaugural address, Havel's talk was an extraordinary jeremiad – eloquent, gentle, but unstinting in its criticism…it was a bracing recitation of urgent needs, an inventory of the damage done to the spirit by 40 years of communist rule…."

In reading Havel's address again, I was struck by the feeling that his message reaches beyond the borders of Czechoslovakia in its applicability.

Following are a few eloquent excerpts:

> Our country is not prospering. The great creative and spiritual potential of our nation is not being used to its fullest….
>
> The worst thing is that we are living in a decayed moral environment. We have become morally ill because we have become accustomed to saying

> one thing and thinking another. We have learned not to believe in anything, not to care about one another and only to look after ourselves. Notions such as love, friendship, compassion, humility and forgiveness have lost their depth and dimension, and for many of us they represent merely some kind of story relic from times past, something rather comical in the era of computers and space rockets....
>
> We must accept this legacy as something which we have brought upon ourselves. If we can accept this, then we will understand that it is up to all of us to do something about it.

Why was this speech compared to Lincoln's second inaugural? I read it again and was reminded of these familiar lines:

> With malice toward none, with charity for all, with firmness in the right as God gives us to see the right, let us strive on to finish the work we are in, to bind up the nation's wounds, to care for him who shall have borne the battle and for his widow and his orphan, to do all which may achieve and cherish a just and lasting peace among ourselves and with all nations.

There is something similar in these speeches to those of the great Greek orators.

Demosthenes charged the men of Athens: "You must not set the example of wrong, either in word or in deed; and you must see to it that our actions, rather than the speeches delivered from this platform, are worthy of our fathers."

Pericles reminded the Athenians, "This empire has been acquired by men who knew their duty and had the courage to do it, who in the hour of conflict had the fear of dishonor always present to them, and who, if ever they failed in an enterprise, would not allow their virtues to be lost to their country."

So what is the common theme in these speeches that spans the centuries? In his book, *Summer Meditations*, Havel wrote, "People need to hear that it makes good sense to behave decently or to help others, to place common interests above their own, to respect the elementary rules of human coexistence."

The real leaders of nations, or of communities, know there is a difference between what people want to hear and what people need to hear.

They also know that words, at times, fall short of reaching the desired goal—unless they lead to action.

Taking Up The Cause

In 1992, the United Nations General Assembly declared 1999 the International Year of Older Persons in an effort to recognize "humanity's demographic coming of age and the promise it holds for maturing attitudes and capabilities in social, economic, cultural and spiritual undertakings." The theme for the year was designated as "Towards a society for all ages."

The gesture was a noble one. The growing cohort of older persons has added years, even decades, of active and useful life to the population. However, the theme should remind us of the expansion of our responsibilities in, not one, but two directions: the old *and* the young. The challenge is not a new one. In his book, *The City in History*, Lewis Mumford writes, "In both Herodotus' account and in those of the archaeologists only one group in the city's life seems hard to spot. Where are the children? … The city, as we first discover it, seems to belong exclusively to the adult population."

When the Athenian statesman, Solon, was called upon to reform oppressive social and economic conditions, he repealed the laws of Dracon and proposed that the measure of a well-governed city was, "That city where those who have not been injured take up the cause of one who has...."

Jim Goldberg is a photographer who has spoken dramatically in behalf of those who have "been injured." In 1997 I visited his photographic exhibit in the San Francisco Museum of Modern Art. Goldberg had spent ten years photographing youth on the streets of San Francisco and Los Angeles. The photographic exhibit of these young runaways was hauntingly titled *Raised by Wolves*; it spoke of 1.4 million teenagers (average age 15) without permanent homes—a modern day echo of Mumford's question of the ages: "Where are the children?"

The plea of Goldberg's exhibit was well stated: "Every child deserves a seamless web of support—made up of parents, friends, neighbors, communities, government, and the private sector—through which no child will slip. It is everyone's responsibility to help weave that web and each of us must do our part."

In the spirit of the U.N. theme of "a society for all ages," very few changes need to be made to the above statement to include senior citizens as well.

There is another reflection—a brighter and more personal one—that comes from the theme "a society for all ages," The U.N. General Assembly also adopted "Principles for Older Persons." Five key words serve as guidelines for program development: independence, participation, care, self-fulfillment, and dignity.

The word "participation" sparked my memory about two of the "heroes" in my community of

Abilene. They were both nationally recognized award winners: ten-year-old Alisia and 88-year-old Walter.

Alisia's three-year-old brother died after a life-long struggle with a variety of illnesses including sixty hospital stays. During the many family hospital visits, Alisia noticed all the other sick children; many of them seemed lonely. So Alisia saved her allowance money and did chores until she got enough money to buy fifteen stuffed animals. Each animal went to a child in the hospital with a note from Alisia that read, "You're somebody special." That was just the beginning—at last count Alisia had collected over 600 stuffed animals for hospitalized children.

The hospital workers were so touched by Alisia's gesture they reported it to the national Make a Difference Day headquarters, which recognized her with a national award.

Early one Sunday morning in 1987, Walter saw a

television program that showed Chinese women sweeping their cities' streets. He was so impressed that, later that morning, he suggested to his Sunday school class that everyone should help keep their city clean. The next morning they began. Walter, who had retired from a distinguished career in university administration, averaged about twelve hours per week retrieving litter, recycling paper, glass and plastic and clearing weeded areas. His efforts were continuing five years later when President George Bush named him (at age 88) a Point of Light and declared June 30, 1992 as Walter's day throughout the nation.

When Walter's daughter was asked to explain his resistance to "retirement," she replied, "He thinks we're put on this Earth to serve others."

People like Alisia and Walter remind me how very important it is for us to remember that in every way we must have a "society for all ages."

THE SIZE OF THE CANVAS

The large multi-colored banner was stretched above the main entrance to the Charleston, South Carolina City Hall. Huge hand-painted letters proclaimed "Spoleto Festival USA." Behind the letters is a wonderful story that bridges the Atlantic.

It began in 1958 when Pulitzer Prize-winning composer Gian Carlo Menotti created a forum in Spoleto, Italy for young Americans interested in the performing arts. It was called the *Festival dei Due Mondi* (Festival of Two Worlds).

Then in 1977 the American counterpart was founded in Charleston, home of both the first theater and first ballet company in America. The Charleston festival runs seventeen days and includes, according to the *Financial Times of London*, "a deliriously eclectic menu spanning opera, chamber and symphonic music, dance, jazz, theatre, art exhibits and, on occasion, puppet shows and circuses."

In 1998 the population of Spoleto, Italy was 37,700 and the Charleston, South Carolina's citizens totaled 100,122—neither could be considered a large city by any standard. Joe Riley, Charleston's long-term mayor, has proper perspective: "Sometimes, if you paint on a smaller canvas, you can make a more beautiful picture." Seeing the city, regardless of size, as a potential work of art is a useful consideration.

Oberammergau, a village of 5,200 in southern Germany, has taken the artistic approach for centuries. Since 1634 the villagers have produced, at the beginning of each decade, a world-famous passion play. Each performance, involving roughly half of the village population, spans the greater part of a day—beginning in the morning, breaking for a lunch intermission, and continuing through the afternoon.

Involvement in the production means so much to the citizens that mortality rates drop in the years just prior to a performance year and then rise in the years following. The number of performances now exceeds 100 during the five-month-long season from May to October. Over half a million visitors, at the rate of 5,000 a day, roughly equal to the city's own population, attend each performance.

Obviously, there are other ways to enhance the city as a work of art. Some of the ways don't require an event, just a simple touch of needed color and beauty.

During the decade of the 1990s, the people of Abilene joined forces to add over 119,000 much-needed trees to our rather barren (except for mesquites) West Texas landscape. One evening during the monthly Artwalk, in the revitalized downtown area, a young lady approached me with an idea. "The trees are nice," Cindy said, "but some color would add so much." She had done her homework and proceeded to tell me how crepe myrtles would not only thrive in the summer heat, but needed little water and provided beautiful red, lavender, and white flowers. With her help, a citywide effort was organized to plant crepe myrtles—at homes, businesses, school and parks. At last count more than 17,000 crepe myrtle plants were adding new color to our city canvas.

Sometimes just one person with an artist's eye can add a touch of beauty to her community, in this case one renewed each year when the crepe myrtles bloom.

MUDVILLE: LIFE IN "A SMALL CITY"

A. Bartlett Giamatti was president of Yale University from 1978 until 1986 when he became president of the National League of Baseball. He then served as Commissioner of Major League Baseball from April 1, 1989 until his death on September 1, 1989. Giamatti wrote, "It has long been my conviction that we can learn far more about the conditions, and values, of a society by contemplating how it chooses to play, to use its free time, to take its leisure, than by examining how it goes about its work."

Giamatti especially loved baseball and believed the sport provided a multi-faceted metaphor for America. In an essay titled *Community,* Giamatti wrote, "...wherever it is and however it is shaped, the sports venue is urban...It is a small city—at once a market, a forum or a meeting place...Indeed, baseball—the most strenuously nostalgic of all our sports…still calls these playing fields, wherever they are, 'parks'…Public places require constant care—they require cleanliness, reasonable order, coherence, and accessibility…so that the energy, the fervent zeal, the rousing excitement, and the happy camaraderie of competition we so value when we come together can continue to flourish for masses of us in the artificial but real confines of that special world…."

Earnest L. Thayer captured for all time the fervent zeal that an entire community can attach to its team's performance when in 1888 he closed his classic poem with the line, "But there is no joy in Mudville—mighty Casey has struck out." Apparently the legendary sports writer Grantland Rice felt a need to revive the perennial sports fan's belief that "there will be another day." In 1906, Rice penned a sequel titled *Casey's Revenge*, which told of the "rematch" of pitcher and batter when "All Mudville had assembled—ten thousand fans had come." The poem closed with these lines:

> Ten thousand hats were thrown in air,
> ten thousand threw a fit,
> But no one ever found the ball
> that mighty Casey hit.
>
> O' somewhere in this favored land
> dark clouds may hide the sun,
> And somewhere bands no longer play
> and children have no fun!
> And somewhere over blighted lives
> there hangs a heavy pall,
> But Mudville hearts are happy now,
> for Casey hit the ball.

Cheering for "our team" can provide a positive pulse for a community. But there are other very real ways that sporting events can play an important role in life outside the arena.

A newspaper clipping dated August 15, 1999 provides an historic example of building community through, as Giamatti said, "how we choose to play."

The article was actually an obituary for a man named Harold Henry Reese. But his nickname had completely supplanted his formal name. The entire baseball world called him "PeeWee." The obituary included his impressive professional career totals with the Dodgers—eight-time All-Star, led Brooklyn to its only World Series championship in 1955 by defeating the Yankees—but several paragraphs were devoted to an accomplishment that surpassed the statistics. They described Reese's friendship with the first man to break professional baseball's color barrier in 1947: "During one particularly tough time when the abuse was getting ugly at Crosley Field in Cincinnati, Reese walked over toward Jackie Robinson and put his arm over the rookie's shoulder, a show of unity from a white to a black that spoke volumes."

"That moment is cited as a turning point in Robinson's transition."

Rachel Robinson, Jackie's wife, described the relationship between the two men by saying they, as "teammates in the truest sense, transcended the hate in their environment and discovered the exhilaration of mutual respect."

A Sight I Will Not Forget

In July 2001 my wife and I traveled to Brady, Texas. The minister didn't refer to the ceremony as a funeral. He called it a celebration of a wonderful woman's life—a life that was filled with family and friends, and loving and giving. He was correct. Even admidst the dark hours of loss, there was much to celebrate for all those who knew her.

Soon we were in our own car and driving toward the cemetery as part of the funeral procession. As we passed through town, the cars approaching us pulled to the side of the road, waiting for the procession to pass. But then I noticed, off to the right, on the main street sidewalk near a big storefront window, a carpenter working outside in the mid-day Texas heat. I watched him as he set his hammer down, turned and faced the procession, head uncovered, hands crossed in front, almost as if at attention. As we drove on, I watched him in the rearview mirror; he didn't move until the procession had passed. Then he picked up his hammer and went back to work. I wondered if he knew the deceased, but decided it was unlikely. I do imagine that he understood pain and loss, because it was obvious by his actions he was a part of the community.

As we drove back to Abilene, I recalled a "letter to the editor" I had clipped and saved from four years earlier. As I re-read it, I realized it really wasn't "to the editor" at all. It was to the people of Abilene:

> "Recently I traveled from central New York to attend a funeral for a very dear and wonderful man. Among the grief of the accident that resulted in his death was a spot that warmed the soul.
>
> When the funeral procession made its way from the church to the cemetery, you as a city paid homage to (our friend) and his loved

ones. It was a sight I will not forget.

As we made our very sad last journey, you stopped to allow our passage. Some were walking, some were in their cars, but you stopped what you were doing. I saw gentlemen remove their hats, and others bow their heads in prayer.

I do not think you realize that at that precise point in time there were no race barriers, no economic barriers, and no age barriers. You were as one. I saw expensive cars and old junkers stop, one behind the other. Young and old, rich and poor, black and white paid their respects to the family, friends and loved ones.

You should be proud of your city and the people who live there. I know others expect this treatment, but to actually see it was awesome. I did want you to know someone noticed and felt the support of the city at a time when it was truly needed."

It was signed,

Syracuse, N.Y.

Perhaps it's important to be reminded that we don't always know when we will have the opportunity to be a meaningful, even if anonymous, part of community.

Section III: STRATEGIES

Strategies, for our purposes, are plans for action. Strategies emerge from our understanding of the existing elements and provide ways for us to realize or improve the way the essential expectations are met. Therefore, the better we understand the existing elements and the more sharply we define the essential expectations, the more apparent the correct strategy will be.

The reflections in this section focus on strategies that are consistent with building stronger community. Five types of strategies are emphasized:

1. Differentiation. Perhaps this is the most important place to begin. In an era of franchises and chain stores there is a tendency for every city to increasingly look like every other city—same restaurants, same hotels, and same retail shops. Added to this is the tendency for workshops, seminars, books, and trade publications to focus on "best practices." Up to a point all of the above can be beneficial and positive—carried too far we promote a "cookie-cutter" syndrome in which a city loses its distinctiveness. In an era of growing travel and tourism, we need to remember that people are attracted to originals, to a city like no other. People generally aren't attracted to copies. The strategy of differentiation emphasizes the importance of remembering the five essential elements of geography, history, demography, heritage, and culture and seeks to draw out from them the ways one's city continues to be unique. In other words, the strategy of trying to copy someone else is of limited usefulness.

Jan Morris captured the essence of the

strategy of differentiation when she wrote, "In Paris I sometimes feel that every street, every event, every gesture is dedicated to some aspect of Parisness!"

2. Renovation. Cities are never finished. Everything eventually wears out, breaks down, or crumbles. Neither the tangible "city" nor the intangible "community" is immune to deteriorating effects of the passing of time. Streets, bridges, neighborhoods, trust, and respect—all can suffer from inattention or neglect; all need periodic renewal. Renovation is vital to the survival of community.

In a sense, renovation is positive change. Restoration, to bring something back to its original form, can be considered a form of renovation. But "renovation" may also include giving a new look or a new life to something old. The first step to successful renovation is to know the difference between the things that should change and the things that should never change.

3. Collaboration. There may have been a time, according to the movies, when rugged independence was the way a town's problems were solved and victories were won. But today, interdependence is the key to community success. Cities progress when people move forward <u>together</u>. The information age has given new meaning to the idea of networking. As Robert Putnam wrote, "The community as a whole will benefit by the cooperation of all its parts."

The challenge today is not simply to "try harder" to make the same old solutions to age-old problems; the challenge today is to look for new combinations of resources—to shape solutions in new ways by bringing new partners into the process. In an era in which business competitors have become partners by creating new alliances, cities must also look for new partnerships with other cities, other levels of government, other organizations, and other groups. Computer era technology will continue to make new collaborations not only possible but also necessary.

4. Circulation. One thing that a city must avoid is stagnation. If the stirring stops, if there is no circulation—there is no life. Circulation is more than communication. Communication can be misunderstood as a press release, or a speech, or a single town hall meeting. Circulation is constantly, continuously flowing.

Circulation is more than a single exchange. In his in-depth study titled *Life in a Mexican Village,* Oscar Lewis wrote, "The circulation of goods in Tepoztlan is carried on by means of the local market, stores, itinerant merchants, inter-village trade, the sale and purchase of goods in Cuernavaca and other large towns, and the exchange and barter of goods between families in the village."

Circulation is more than the movement of vehicular traffic. It is captured by Ray Bradbury when he described the similar phenomenon in both a small-town plaza in Mexico and in the cosmopolitan city-center of Paris, where even in miserable weather, "generations gather to talk and stare." But, Bradbury suggests, there are places in America that have "forgotten how to gather." The sidewalks and the "walkability" of a downtown are important for circulation. Town squares and plazas, places to gather, are important for circulation—and circulation is important to the health of the community.

5. Celebration. There are a lot of things wrong in our cities today—but there are a lot of things right. Elected officials and non-elected leaders in every area of the city have a responsibility to plan regularly for celebrations.

Parades, festivals, sporting events, and concerts are just some of the ways a city celebrates. And these celebrations don't always have to be big and expensive. One of my favorite celebration days in Abilene is the Fourth of July. Thousands of people gather for the fireworks display; but during the day several neighborhoods have their own parades where the kids decorate their bicycles, wagons—even pets!—and everyone, young and old, celebrates community.

HOW TO BE "AT HOME IN THE WORLD"

One phrase in the report leaped off the page.

The entire report concerning an associate's visit to an out-of-town organization was positive and informative, but one phrase in its simplicity was succinctly profound. He wrote, "The well-kept landscaping gave an indication of caring." The report was not praising the landscaping but praising the caring attitude that was symbolized through the landscaping.

Unfortunately, a high quality of caring is a rare commodity in this age of fast-paced, computerized living. Yet there continues to exist within most, if not all, of us a genuine appreciation for even the smallest signs of authentic caring. That's what the well-kept landscaping symbolizes—but the signs can be so subtle and so varied—such as thoroughly clean tables at a restaurant, or a warm, personal voice answering the phone.

Sinclair Lewis provided a descriptive picture of a place where the lack of caring was apparent. In his *Main Street*, a first impression of the little town of Gopher Prairie was depicted in the following way:

"It was not only the unsparing unapologetic ugliness and the rigid straitness which overwhelmed her. It was the planlessness, the flimsy temporariness of the buildings, their faded unpleasant colors. The street was cluttered with electric-light poles, telephone poles, gasoline pumps for motor cars, boxes of goods."

The next sentence supplies the underlying root of the problem: "Each man had built with the most valiant disregard of all the others."

In an age when expressions such as "I could care less!" and "See if I care!" are heard all too often, an easy way for an employee, an organization, or a city to rise above the others is to develop a solid reputation as one who has developed the capacity for caring—or a valiant regard of others.

In 1971 Milton Mayeroff wrote a thoughtful book titled, *On Caring*, in which he suggests, "in the sense in which a man can ever be said to be at home in the world, he is at home not through dominating, or explaining, or appreciating, but through caring and being cared for."

Mayeroff discusses several "major ingredients of caring." Three ingredients, which may help to explain why the quality of caring is not more abundant, are patience, courage, and selflessness. To care means truly giving of one's self, one's time, and perhaps at times even to venture into the unknown. Caring, by its very nature, moves the focus away from self to someone else.

As customers, we like to do business with the company that seems to really care about us; as neighbors, we prefer to live around others whom we perceive genuinely to care about us; as citizens, we prize the leaders who truly care about people—in all three instances the message is the same: "Don't just *tell* me how you care; instead, look for ways to *show* me how much you care!"

One of the first and most conclusive ways a church, a school, a city, or any human organization is differentiated is based on the quality of caring. It only takes a few minutes to begin to determine whether "they care" or "they don't care." And caring comes through in so many different ways—patience, well-kept landscapes, and a high regard for others.

THE GREATEST WORK OF ART POSSIBLE

They were the only words engraved on the small bronze plate. One single sentence: "A city is the greatest work of art possible."

It was almost dark as we left the Town Hall in Sydney, Australia—but off to the left, barely visible in the dusk, was a bronze bust of a man on a granite pillar. Closer inspection revealed his identity: Lloyd Rees, 1895—1988, Australian Artist. Nothing else—nothing but his nine word statement—"A city is the greatest work of art possible."

Over the decade of the 1990s, I had the great privilege to observe a dramatic transformation take place in Abilene, Texas. Looking back over those years, four insights seem to emerge pertaining to the topic of cultural tourism.

- **A first insight: Great works of art attract tourists.**

I had never thought of a city as a potential work of art until that night in Sydney, as I stood only a short distance from that world-recognized symbol of cultural beauty—the Sydney Opera House. It is important to remember that tourists don't go to cities by accident; they must be attracted—and great art attracts tourists. As important as a strong economy is, it alone is not a magnet that will attract visitors. Neither a city nor a nation can thrive solely on a strong economy. There must be something to nurture the spirit of community.

- **A second insight: Discover the distinctive.**

Visitors to the abandoned ruins of Ephesus, Turkey are told by the guides that they are walking among the most complete set of ruins of any ancient city and yet, they say, it is believed that perhaps twice as much of the city still remains unexcavated.

In some ways, our cities today are not unlike Ephesus. Over the years, the sands of time have buried so much of our history and heritage. Treasures have been lost; artifacts have been misplaced; buildings have been demolished; once-told stories have been forgotten. In each city and town, there should be an ongoing program of cultural excavation and discovery. We have lost much of what makes each city distinctive.

It is not the ways in which we are alike that attract the cultural tourist; it is the ways we are different, unique, and original. If we copy some other city, we are doing it wrong. Tourists travel to see original works of art, not copies.

A man once told me he remembered Abilene from his one visit, several years prior, because there was a railroad track that ran right through the center of town. That was all he remembered. And for too many years, we considered that aesthetically challenged railroad to be nothing more than an unfortunate eyesore.

Now we see it as a positive part of our identity. Literally hundreds of trees line the track which now serves as a long, green, linear park. The three railroad buildings have been completely restored. One building is the new home of a chocolate candy maker, and the depot now contains the Visitor Center, the offices of the Abilene Convention and Visitor Bureau, and the Abilene Cultural Affairs Council. The old railroad hotel across the street now houses the Museums of Abilene—a fine art museum, a children's museum, and an historical museum. Little more than a block away is the beautifully restored Paramount Theatre, which shows a year-long schedule of classic films.

The arts have played the leading role in the transformation of downtown. Every month, on the second Thursday, hundreds of Abilenians and their guests stroll the streets during Artwalk, when as many as 14 different venues open new exhibits. In addition to the museums and galleries, the venues include bank lobbies, jewelry stores, and other retail businesses. In this same area, a spring arts and railroad festival called "Celebrate Abilene" annually acknowledges our birth in 1881 as a railroad town. At the beginning of the last decade, there was *one* place for a visitor to eat in downtown Abilene—ten years later there are a *dozen*. More than 40 different buildings have been a part of the downtown transformation.

- **A third insight: "In every city there is some new thing that waits to be done with distinction."**

James Michener wrote many wonderful works of fiction including his Pulitzer Prize winning *South Pacific*. But from one of his few non-fiction works, entitled *The Quality of Life*, comes this challenging statement: "In every city there is some new thing that waits to be done with distinction."

Great art is often the result of new ideas done with distinction. Today, painting a ceiling is not a particularly remarkable nor novel idea. But Michelangelo executed the idea with such distinction that for almost 500 years tourists by the thousands have traveled to Rome to view the Sistine Chapel. Every year we see evidence that tourists can be attracted to new things done with distinction.

A few years ago a children's book titled *Santa Calls* was published. The nationally acclaimed children's author and illustrator, William Joyce, told the fictional story of three children and their personal encounter with Santa. In this book, the children's hometown just happened to be Abilene, Texas. That simple serendipity was the beginning of a project which some talented and dedicated folks set about to do with distinction.

Today, Abilene is the home of the National Center for Children's Illustrated Literature. Each year the National Center presents exhibits featuring original works from award-winning children's books. The exhibits then go on tour to cities throughout the country, including museums in places such as Houston, Dallas, and Indianapolis. As a result, thousands of elementary school children are developing an early appreciation for art and art exhibits. They are also spending more time with books, and the younger ones are enjoying more books read to them by parents and grandparents. A beautiful bronze sculpture depicting the three children from *Santa Calls* now graces the newly landscaped park in the center of town.

The great idea done with distinction does more than attract visitors—it pulls the community together and it lifts people up—it inspires, nourishes, and enlightens.

- **A fourth insight: Cultural tourism is a non-exclusive industry.**

While only a few fortunate cities may be selected for the final site locations for large manufacturing industries, every city, regardless of size, is free to build its own tourism enterprise. And since travel and tourism is such a large and rapidly-growing industry, each city has the opportunity to find ways to become a destination tourism site or, at least, play a supporting role.

Tourism can have a synergistic effect. The more that each city enhances its own attractiveness to tourists, the more all cities in the region and beyond potentially benefit. There is so much to work with—dramatic history, a rich, colorful heritage, and the awareness that the size of the city canvas does not determine the quality of the work of art.

HALLMARKS OF EXCELLENCE

The appointment at Hallmark Cards' corporate offices was at 8 a.m.

Unfamiliar with the Kansas City morning traffic, I overcompensated and arrived 25 minutes early. Walking through the halls, I noticed a surprising amount of activity, considering the time of day.

Many employees were already at work, apparently not because they had miscalculated the necessary travel time, but because exceptional levels of performance are characteristic of the way they do things at this remarkable company.

High performance is nothing new for Hallmark. Occasional spurts of high quality performance are generally enough to distinguish an individual or organization from the mass of mediocrity. But at Hallmark, excellence has been a way of life, for more than three-quarters of a century, under the exemplary leadership of two generations.

J.C. Hall founded the company in 1910 in Kansas City. For 56 years this "benevolent patriarch" meticulously monitored the quality of every item in the product line. He personally gave final approval to each new card with the shorthand code, "O.K.J.C."

But the story of Hallmark Cards is not simply the story of one man—it is the story of a family, a family that consists of thousands of full-time employees, a family that publishes millions of greeting cards each working day, a family that prints cards in many languages and distributes them in more than 100 countries.

One member of this family, an employee named Ed Goodman, made an exceptional contribution in 1944 when he captured the spirit of the company by penning the phrase, "When you care enough to send the very best."

The reason for Hallmark's reputation for quality

becomes more obvious after visiting with members of the Hallmark "family," watching them energetically go about their work, listening to them enthusiastically describe their co-workers as "patient, nurturing, and nice." Perhaps it is best expressed in a unique Hallmark card—a card not sold in any Hallmark store—a card that was distributed only to the employees during the company's 75th year—a card containing the collaborative efforts of a group of Hallmark employees:

For us excellence
is an aspiration,
an attitude,
a pursuit...
a way of life.

Excellence is all of us
working together, aspiring to
the fullness of our potential,
always in pursuit of higher standards—
determined to do
everything we do somehow better

than it ever has been done before.

Excellence is found
in the caring,
in the trying,
in the doing.

It is our objective.
We seek it
with dedication.
It is the hallmark
of this corporation.

In their book, *In Search of Excellence*, Tom Peters and Robert Waterman remind us of the importance of creating "pockets of excellence." The determined efforts and great expectations of a few persistent people can have an amazing effect upon the level of excellence within a company or a community.

A "COURAGEOUS" COMMUNITY

For eighteen months Jonathan Wright took on a challenging assignment. He began to commute from his home in West Conshohocken, Pennsylvania to spend about half of each month in Hawaii, because as he said, "I had unfinished business with the Australians." Jon Wright is a mainsheet trimmer. The 1987 competition was the fifth time that he and Dennis Conner had sailed for the America's Cup.

The story of Stars and Stripes' smashing victory over Kookaburra III was well-documented in the American media—but the story of the disciplined dedication of the eleven determined men who sailed to success is not as familiar.

Shortly after he returned to his sailboat business in West Conshohocken, Wright graciously agreed to recount for me his memories of recapturing the Cup. It was "the greatest win ever," he said, "because we got up off the canvas and went down there and won it back." As the mainsheet trimmer, Wright controls the sail, which is "the engine" of the boat. While Conner is steering the boat, Wright adjusts the balance of the boat with the sails to keep it at optimum speed.

My primary interest was to gain insight into the motivation behind these history-making heroics.

"To be honest with you," Wright said, "it was a ho-hum event for 32 years, because the Cup was kept in the New York Yacht Club and the public never saw it. Every three years somebody would come and try to win it, but we would always win. But when the Australians invented a better mousetrap with the winged keel—all of a sudden, we Americans got very upset. Someone had taken something away from us—not from the New York Yacht Club, but from our country."

"The fact that we lost it" was probably the single

factor that contributed most to the motivation. But this particular motivation had a name. It was called "commitment to the commitment."

Wright explained this phrase coined by the skipper, Dennis Conner, by saying, "It was bigger than just saying, 'Yeah, I'll be there at 5:30,' it was a year and a half out of a guy's life. It's one thing to just go out there and go through the motions, but we were driven—we were driven by one goal. The new guys saw how driven Dennis and I were to get the Cup back. We were a part of losing the Cup, which had been a big part of my life."

America's Cup wasn't won in four days at Fremantle. The America's Cup was won during eighteen months of premeditated preparation. The crew gave meaning to American management guru Peter Drucker's observation that if goals are only good intentions, they are worthless. Goals must "degenerate into work." That work was performed with an intensity that Wright had not seen in the preparation for the previous four Cups, primarily because of one factor—something had been lost.

In business and personal life, a renewal of energy and interest is essential after something of value has been lost. Some companies have found a similar method of motivation that attempts to avoid the pain of loss. They ask each employee to make every decision, take every action, and treat every person as if they were on the verge of losing every customer.

The spirit of community is a fragile thing. If taken for granted, it can wilt and rapidly wane. The spirit of community is always "unfinished business" and thus needs constant attention from a network of people who are willing to forego trophy cups or personal acclaim, people who understand clearly what "commitment to the commitment" means, and even more what it demands.

There is a special word for those people who can

sustain their commitment to the community through the bad times as well as the good—they're called "volunteers."

The Symbolic Skyline

"A city of ancient churches and cathedrals thrusting their hallowed spires and towers against the skyline"—it's a line that could describe so many cities but it happens to have been written about Dublin, Ireland.

The architecture of church buildings is such a defining part of so many city skylines and even more important is the influential role that churches play within our community.

When the great fire of 1666 destroyed so many buildings in London, many churches were destroyed. Christopher Wren, Britain's greatest architect, was commissioned to design and supervise the rebuilding of fifty-one church buildings over the next forty-six years; London was not to be without its churches.

In Robert Putnam's book *Bowling Alone*, he

reports that three-quarters of the U.S. workforce said that "the breakdown in community" and "selfishness" were problems of major concern. Further into his analysis, Putnam states that "Faith communities in which people worship together are arguably the single most important repository of social capital in America." He continues, "As a rough rule of thumb, our evidence shows, nearly half of all associational memberships in America are church related, half of all volunteering occurs in a religious context." He concludes, "How involved we are in religion today matters a lot for America's social capital."

Putnam uses the term "social capital" to refer to the "connections among individuals…and the norms of reciprocity and trustworthiness." Later in his expansive study, he summarizes "religion is today, as it has traditionally been, a central fount of American community life and health." In addition to the services provided to community members, Putnam suggests there are indirect benefits such as "nurturing civic skills, inculcating moral values, and encouraging altruism."

Without stretching the point too far, there are some similarities between family and community. A. Bartlett Giamatti has written, "If a family is an expression of continuing through biology, a city is an expression of continuing through will and imagination." Therefore, some insights for building stronger communities might be gained by thinking in terms of family.

In Royce Money's book, *Building Stronger Families*, he cites a national study which surfaced six qualities consistently found in strong families: (1) Appreciation was frequently expressed; (2) Good communication patterns existed; (3) Time was spent together; (4) Commitment was cultivated through respect, trust, and acceptance; (5) Crises were dealt with positively; and (6) Firm spiritual values provided a moral base.

Author James Michener in his non-fiction work, *This Noble Land*, echoed the importance of this sixth quality. One chapter was devoted to defining a "noble land," in which Michener isolated thirteen characteristics, each phrased in the form of a question. Question nine asked, "Does the nation provide churches for the moral guidance of its people and especially its leaders?" Michener concludes this section with the following observation: "I would never want to live in a community that did not have influential churches."

The skylines of our cities would be sadly lacking if the spires and towers of the church buildings were suddenly gone, but how much weaker and more fractured would our communities be if the immeasurable impact of the churches should disappear?

Knowing What to Look For

Our ultimate destination was Nashville, a little more than two hundred miles ahead if we just stayed on Interstate 40.

But as we arrived at Memphis, we turned north on Highway 51. About an hour later, we pulled off the highway and onto the streets of Henning, Tennessee. I had wanted to make this visit for several years. There were some things I wanted to see with my own eyes. Alex Haley had visited Abilene in 1987. As he and I visited, I was engrossed in his story about the writing of the Pulitzer Prize-winning *Roots*—his own personal journey to discover the people and places that had preceded him. When he died, he was working on his next book, which was to be titled *Henning*; it was intended to be recollections of his hometown.

There were three things I especially wanted to see:

First was his house. It is still much as it was when Haley was a boy and it served as the anchoring point for his early years. This was the home of "Grandpa" Will Palmer and "Grandma" Cynthia Palmer; their daughter, Bertha, had married Simon Alexander Haley. While Simon was doing graduate work at Cornell University, Bertha and baby boy, Alex, stayed with her parents.

We walked slowly through each room of the house, as the tour guide provided helpful insights into this place that had housed three generations. But the rooms, although the source of many interesting stories, were not my primary interest. We then went outside and stood on the porch. This was the place; it was here that young Alex's journey had begun. In *Roots*, Haley revealed:

> ...they had names like Aunt Plus,

> Aunt Liz, Aunt Till, Aunt Viney and Cousin Georgia. With the supper dishes washed, they all would go out on the front porch and sit in cane-bottomed rocking chairs, and I would be among them and sort of scrunch myself down behind the white-painted rocker holding Grandma...always they would talk about the same things—snatches and patches of what later I'd learn was the long, cumulative family narrative that had been passed down across the generations.

A plaque near the steps of the front porch reads, "*Roots* was born on this front porch. Summer after summer, as I grew up, my Grandma and my great aunts told our family's treasured story all the way back to the African who said his name was Kinte."

Just two blocks away, around a corner, was the

second sight on my list. The original building had been renovated and enlarged over the past eighty years. But it was still on the same site and still serving the same purpose. This building had been host to a very important event for Alex Haley's family but also an historic event for the town. Again from *Roots*, Haley wrote about the marriage of his mother and father: "Their wedding in the New Hope CME Church in the summer of 1920 was Henning's first social event attended by both black and white."

My third objective was to visit Alex Haley's grave. He is buried in the front yard, just a few steps away from the porch. I had heard there was a particular statement he had wanted inscribed on his tombstone. As I stood at the foot of his grave, I noted it expressed the essence of Haley's discovery—and an important key to building family and to building community—in six short words: "Find the Good and Praise It."

The Pickering Perspective

Within the span of a few hours, I was reminded that contemporary life could still reach back across the centuries and benefit from ancient Greek legend.

The evening news was drawing the day to a close as a reporter visited one of the baseball spring training camps. He asked the general manager if any personnel surprises had developed during the weeks of workouts.

"Not really," the general manager replied, "everyone performed about like I expected they would."

Less than an hour earlier, my wife and I had been watching the 1938 movie, *Pygmalion.* George Bernard Shaw received an Academy Award for best screenplay for this black-and-white film classic, adapted from his 1912 play of the same name.

According to Greek legend, Pygmalion was a

sculptor who carved an ivory statue of a beautiful woman and then fell in love with it. In answer to his prayer, the statue became a living woman named Galatea whom Pygmalion married.

In Shaw's modern version of this legend, London Professor Henry Higgins, with help from Colonel Pickering, undertakes the challenge of transforming a Cockney flower girl named Eliza Doolittle into a duchess.

In 1964 Lerner and Loewe adapted the story into the musical *My Fair Lady*, which won eight Academy Awards including the Oscar for best film of the year.

The ancient Greek legend of Pygmalion, with all its variations, has a timeless quality. Its appeal, at least in part, must be related to the excitement of seeing someone realize his or her full potential.

One brief exchange between Eliza Doolittle and Professor Higgins provides an important insight into the crucial role that others play in helping one become the best he or she can be:

Higgins: "My manners are exactly the same as Colonel Pickering's."

Eliza: "That's not true. He treats a flower girl as if she was a duchess."

Higgins: "And I treat a duchess as if she was a flower girl."

The message is universal. It applies to baseball general managers and managers of all kinds. It also applies to coaches, teachers, parents—all who are in roles of leadership in their community.

People respond according to the way they are treated—and people are treated according to the expectations one has of them. That is probably why the general manager hadn't been surprised by his players' performances.

Expanding on Eliza's observation, we appear to have three options:

Option One: We can treat flower girls as flower girls and duchesses as duchesses.

Option Two: We can treat both flower girls and duchesses as flower girls.

Unfortunately, far too often one of the above choices is selected. But if we want to allow every individual to reach their full potential, we will prefer the third choice which is:

Option Three: We can treat both flower girls and duchesses as duchesses.

The Meeting Place

In July of 1891, Theodore C. Link's architectural firm, Link and Cameron, won the first prize of $10,000 in a national design competition for a new railroad station. The Romanesque style was intended to "herald the grandeur" of St. Louis and was said to have been inspired by the walled city of Carcasonne in Southern France.

Three years later, on September 2, 1984, the first train pulled into Union Station, which covered slightly more than 100 acres, including the largest train shed in the world.

Rail travel continued to increase into the 1900s, and travelers from all directions headed to St. Louis for the World's Fair of 1904. The country was singing "Meet Me in St. Louis, Louis" and Union Station was the meeting place.

Peacetime traffic reached its peak in 1920, when

the station averaged a staggering 269 trains per day. During the 1920s, additional tracks were added. With a new total of 42 tracks, Union Station became the railroad station with the greatest number of tracks on one level anywhere in the world.

During World War II, the facilities of Union Station were stretched to their limits by servicemen and their families making cross-country connections. The peak year of this era was 1943, when 22 million passengers passed through the portals.

Through all the excitement of the first 40 years of the 20th century, it was difficult to realize that transportation itself was transitioning as well. In Norbury L. Wayman's *St. Louis Union Station and Its Railroads*, he isolates a very important statistic; in 1900, railroads carried 84 percent of all intercity passengers, but by 1954, 88 percent of travelers were going by private automobile.

The grand old station was slowly being drained

of its life and vitality. Then Amtrak injected new but short-lived hope in the early 1970s.

October 1978 must have been the darkest month in the history of Union Station. On the last day of the month, the last train, an Amtrak to Chicago, pulled out. In the same month, this historic structure with its 230-foot clock tower came dangerously close to demolition because of a disappointing redevelopment venture.

But, after seven years of silence, Union Station re-emerged as a center of excitement in St. Louis. The Grand Hall now serves as the lobby of a 500-room luxury hotel; nestled under the expansive Union Station roof are over 100 specialty shops and restaurants. People by the thousands are returning to this monument that possesses so many memories of a past era. Union Station is, once again, a meeting place.

What makes stories like this so important is that

Union Station represents the exception to the general rule. Alvin Toffler, in his book *Future Shock*, suggested that we have become conditioned by a paper-plate and plastic-cup mentality and have become, to a disturbing extent, a "throwaway society." Everything is treated as if it were temporary.

It is important to remember there are some things and some relationships that are worth keeping, even protecting. In this world caught up with change, perhaps the toughest decisions we face are those that involve determining what to throw away and what to keep. Union Station stands as a nice reminder that there are some things worth keeping.

The Visible (and Invisible) Effects of Time

The city started as a Roman legionnaires' camp in the early years of the Roman Empire. Some buildings still stand that were mentioned in the documents of the 12th and 13th centuries. Walking the streets of Vienna, it is difficult to imagine that this city suffered a great fire in 1258. After rebuilding from that catastrophe, the city sustained an even greater blow during World War II. Some have estimated that as much as 40 percent of the city's buildings was either destroyed or seriously damaged through the bombings and Nazi occupation.

After an extensive period of rebuilding and repairing, this city has once again risen out of the ashes and ruins. The people of Vienna refuse to accept defeat; they have overcome fire, wars, and economic depression. The majestic buildings of

Vienna, old and new, stand as a monument to citizens who were determined to overcome any threats to their city and rise above them in the spirit of renewal.

After Bob Waterman co-authored the best-selling book *In Search of Excellence* with Tom Peters, he wrote a follow-up book titled *The Renewal Factor.* The following statement taken from the preface serves as a premise for the book: "No organization can maintain excellence without renewing. No organization can strive for excellence, or even attempt to improve, without the ability to renew."

While Waterman was writing with the business organization primarily in mind, his observation is no less applicable for a community. Renewal is the antidote for obsolescence, decay, and apathy.

Even when things seem to be going well we must be concerned about the invisible yet acid-like effects of complacency which slowly eat away at the very foundations of community.

In his book, *On Leadership*, John W. Gardner, former U.S. Secretary of Health, Education, and Welfare, writes "Values always decay over time." Communities that keep their values alive should always remember that no matter how persistent the process of decay, it can be overcome by having an even stronger process for renewal.

TWELVE QUALITIES OF COMMUNITY

What are the factors that make a quality community? Everyone would, no doubt, have their own list, but I would like to propose twelve. To each of the twelve points, I will attach a quote which encapsulizes the thought and serves as an anchor to which we can tie.

Before I get to the twelve points, however, I want to open with one introductory thought. Some of you may be familiar with the works of Wendell Berry. He is a thoughtful writer on the importance of community. In an airport not long ago, I ran across his latest book titled *Jayber Crow*, which is a novel about a man and his community. The book contains this statement: "What I saw now was the community imperfect and irresolute but held together by the frayed and always fraying, incomplete and yet ever-holding bonds of the various sorts of affection." I thought to myself "that describes all our communities" and establishes the context for all who serve as custodians of their communities. We have the responsibility of dealing with this imperfect thing called "community" and the bonds that hold us together in the community. But the bonds are frayed and they will continue to fray. Our challenge is to continue to hold that community together and to make it stronger.

With that thought in mind, let us look at twelve factors that influence community:

1. Clear Identity. We have all heard the comments that people would rather live "someplace" than "anyplace." We all want to feel as if we are living in some place that has a sense of identity. To clarify who we are, four of the very best places to look would be our geography, our demography, our history, and our heritage. We need to continually study them and interpret their implications.

Part of our job sometimes may be that of an explorer who continues to discover his true identity, or her unique place. All people want to feel they belong to something about which they can feel good; that is part of our job in clarifying the identity of our community.

Claire Gaudiani wrote, "Successful communities share a common story and a common set of beliefs as much as they share a common set of goals or activities." We spend a lot of time working on our goals. Every year we talk about our goals, but it is just as important for us to understand our story—and every place has a different history and a different heritage. Of all the cities and towns in the world there are no two that have exactly the same history, exactly the same heritage, exactly the same demography, and exactly the same geography—and therein lies the key to uniqueness.

2. Positive Change. Although James Michener is best known for his novels, he has also written some non-fiction; one of those works was titled *The Quality of Life.* In that book, among a lot of other helpful thoughts, he writes, "In every city there is some great idea waiting to be done with distinction." That phrase has both a positive and a negative side to it. Isn't it tragic to think of all the cities that have had a great idea waiting to be done, but the idea has never been developed, never implemented, still waiting?

The positive side is thinking that in every single city, there is the potential of some great idea—something that will make a big difference. Just imagine the dynamic impact when a *great* idea is done with distinction.

But doing new things implies change. One of our responsibilities as leaders of a city is to know there are things that need to change and there are some things that should never change. The key is to know which is which.

3. Constant Renewal. Even the "best of things" needs occasional renewal. John Gardner in his book *On Leadership* states, "Values always decay over time. Societies that keep their values alive do so not by escaping the process of decay but by powerful processes of regeneration." To tighten the focus for our purposes we only need to take the word "societies" out and put the word "communities" in its place.

Everything decays over time. So we have at least a two-pronged challenge of renewal. One is the renewal of facilities, or the physical component of the city. We could say one is the renewal of the visible, and one is the renewal of the invisible. Every time we allow an old building that was a part of our history, our heritage, and our community to decay, deteriorate, and eventually be destroyed, we let go of a part of our past; additionally, we may even be sending a message about values.

We can never go back again. We cannot resurrect those old buildings. When something is gone, it is gone forever and can never be restored. We need to see that someone is busily giving attention to how we can know that in the passing of the torch from one generation to another the things that we value aren't lost.

If we value the spirit of community, then we must be sure that it is safely passed on to the next generation.

4. Attractive Center. I use that first word intentionally—attractive—because attractive suggests pulling, a drawing power. In several different works over the years, the city is referred to as a magnet. Rosabeth Moss Kanter, in one of her books, talks about a city that is really both magnet and glue. It is the magnet to pull; but then it has to be the glue to hold after it has attracted. We must ask ourselves, "How are we continuing to keep our strength as a magnet to attract and yet at the same time being the kind of glue that keeps people together?"

John Ruskin said, "We require from buildings, as from men, two kinds of goodness: first, doing their practical duty well; then that they be graceful and pleasing in doing it." We know that beauty attracts, don't we? It is just as true in the city as it is in any context. In the same way that a beautiful centerpiece on a table sets the tone for the entire table, I really believe every city or town has to have a center somewhere. Some place there has to be a center, and that center needs to be attractive—both attractive in the sense of being appealing and attractive in the sense that it pulls people toward it.

5. Congenial Design. A cousin to the previous factor is this one—a congenial design says "This is a warm and friendly place." In some cities I visit, I feel immediately welcomed and accepted, while in others I find that it is hard to find my way around—it just doesn't seem to work and things just don't seem to fit and flow. Ray Bradbury, the science fiction writer, has also written a book on city design called *Yestermorrow*. He writes, "Give the community back to the community, to build a base for young and old, and discourage the endless miles of mindless driving as millions of people pass other millions looking for Somewhere To Go."

Congenial design means there needs to be a place that is friendly, a place people feel comfortable, a place that is accessible. I think a key question is, "Is it walkable?" I almost think that is a kind of test for congenial design. If you can't take people on a walking tour, if there is not someplace, hopefully downtown, that we can take people on a walking tour, maybe we need to find a way to make that happen. There needs to be a walkable component to cities so people can get out of their cars; cities were not ever intended to be primarily designed for automobiles; cities were first designed for people and they still ought to be for people first. And people need to be able to walk in their cities.

6. Planned Celebration. In every city there ought to be a place for planned celebration. A few years ago I was leading a group on a European tour. We were in Salzburg one night and walked out after dinner to find people crowding the streets. They were getting ready to have a night parade. I told the group, "Isn't this fortunate? We're here on the night they're having a parade!"

A couple of nights later, we were in Lucerne and people were out on the streets. They were getting ready to have a fireworks display over Lake Lucerne. Again I said to the group, "Aren't we lucky? Everywhere we go we're there the night they're having a celebration." In reality, they just seem to celebrate more in the European cities—they're always having parades, fireworks, festivals, and planned celebrations. They do the same things families do. Families have planned celebrations—holidays, birthdays, and anniversaries—and cities should as well.

If we want people to come together, we need a place to have planned celebrations. The city square or plaza serves that purpose well. Samuel Johnson said, "The applause of a single human being is of great consequence." In cities we need to find ways to give applause.

It is so easy for us to focus on the bad—on what the crime rate is and how to decrease homelessness. We could sometimes think our whole job is dealing with problems. While we cannot ignore the problems, we need to be sure that in our community we are going to be spending some time in celebration.

7. Visible Future. People don't want to live in a place that has no future. Once again from John

Gardner's book *On Leadership*: "The first and last task of a leader is to keep hope alive."

My wife will tell you that the first thing we do when we drive into a new town is try to find the center of the city. I just start driving until we find it. Sometimes we find it quickly, and sometimes we are not sure if we ever found it. The first thing a doctor is likely to do in a health evaluation is to check one's heart. The first thing I do to find out about the health of a city is to check its heart—the center of the city.

If the center of the city is vibrant and alive, I feel pretty good about that city. It seems to be a city with a future—a city that feels good about itself. However, if I go into the center of the city and I find boarded windows, closed doors and empty streets, I get a different feeling.

Gardner says there is such a thing as the visible future—it is not a guess. If you plant seedlings you can say there will be a forest here some day—that is a visible future.

But if you haven't done anything, if you haven't planted anything, then who knows what the future will be?

The second part of this—and I began to feel this increasingly with every year of the nine years I served as mayor—is the children. If you want to know what your city's future looks like, you'd better see what is happening with the children. If the children are saying, "As soon as I get old enough I'm leaving this place," that tells you something about the future; but if the children are saying, "I love this place. This is where my grandparents and parents live and this is where I want to raise my children," you have a visible future that can be very bright.

8. Inclusive Participation. I put those two words together on purpose because even when we just *talk* about participation, we can be selective and sometimes exclusive. If we really want a quality community, we need *inclusive* participation.

I agree with Frances Hesselbein, former head of the National Girl Scouts Association: "The day of partnership is upon us, and these new parnerships can become the engine that drives the renewal of community."

9. External Energy. With all this focus on the city we cannot think with a mentality of isolationism. We have to make sure we stay connected to the outside world. Rosabeth Moss Kanter, whom I mentioned earlier, said we must "attract a flow of external resources—new people or new companies—to renew and expand skills, broaden horizons, and hold up a comparative mirror against world standards." There has to be a way to continue to keep connected to the rest of the world.

In reality, there is only one economy today; that is the world economy. There is no such thing as an exclusively local economy or pure state economy—there is just a world economy, of which we are all part.

People continually look for new places to go and new adventures and ways to spend their time. So the tourism dollar is open and available, but it is more open and available to the places that have those characteristics about which we have already talked: a clear identity of who they are, who are really in touch with their history and their heritage, their geography, and their demography. Additionally, they must be well connected to their surroundings and to the rest of the world.

10. Disciplined Balance. Francis Fukuyama wrote the following: "Americans are so used to celebrating their own individualism and diversity that they sometimes forget that there can be too much of a good thing. Both American democracy and American business have been successful because they partook of individualism and community simultaneously."

This kind of balance means realizing that our challenge of providing services to the community is not simply to provide *individual* services—not just to see that trash is picked up, for example, but also to see that we're providing for the needs of the collective *group* of people. There must be balance there. If we can create an atmosphere within our community that says, "If I help make things better for all of us, they'll be better for me as well. If I help make this a safer community for the neighborhood, it is also going to be a safer community for me."

In the last few years we have heard a lot about a bumper sticker mentality that said, "It's the economy, Stupid." I would like to counterbalance that with a bumper sticker that says it is not just the economy—"it's the community."

11. Purposeful Circulation. Vaclav Havel, president of the Czech Republic, wrote: "I must repeat certain things aloud over and over again...the dormant goodwill in people needs to be stirred... Goodwill longs to be recognized and cultivated." I think every public official ought to have this quote somewhere on his or her desk as a reminder. This is what I mean by circulation—there has to be a "stirring." If water is not flowing it becomes stagnant. Communities can become stagnant for the same reason. They need to be vital and lively; so there must be a constant stirring.

Purposeful circulation says, "I am going to decide the things that are most important to talk about and I am going to keep talking about them." Every mayor, city official or city manager ought to think about the two or three things that need constant attention and keep stirring them. This is the way to send signals about what is important.

Another form of circulation is captured in the little sign, which says, "A desk is a terrible place from which to observe what is really going on." Time spent in the office should be counterbalanced by time spent out among the people—circulating purposefully.

12. Passionate Leaders. Elie Wiesel in his book, *And the Sea is Never Full*, said it about as well as it can be said: "Surely, when human lives are involved, indifference is not an answer." There *must* be somebody who cares. If the mayor, city officials, and city manager are not people who genuinely care about what happens to the people who live in their community, then the wrong people are in those spots.

We've come full circle and returned to the opening quote: "What I saw now was the community imperfect and irresolute but held together by the frayed and always fraying, incomplete and yet everholding bonds of the various sorts of affection"—people who really love their communities, people who really love their hometowns. When those people are in positions of leadership and responsibility, they tend to make better decisions for all of us—for the entire community.

Post Script

September 30, 2001 –

(The last day of an unforgettable month)

The finished manuscript for this book was submitted to the publisher in August. Now, as I review the galley proofs, the world has changed. No one has emerged unaffected, untouched. No matter how far away from New York City we may have been on September 11, we felt the impact—and it was real and personal.

News media provided continuing reports, but an e-mail from Brandon provided Sylvia and me with our most personal connection to that tragic day. Brandon grew up in our neighborhood. (His parents, Ken and Connie, cherished friends, live only a few blocks away.) After completing college, Brandon officed on the 22nd floor of the New York Stock Exchange building. Brandon is safe and we are grateful—but his e-mail reverberated with the feelings of one who was an eyewitness to a time when the safety of so many was exploited.

A few brief passages from his account of "the most extraordinary morning of my life:"

> Others on my floor rushed into my office and we stood for a few seconds trying to comprehend what we were looking at...Once the flames died down a little bit, we could see the huge gash in the side of the building. Smoke was pouring from the building and the sky was full of papers, flying everywhere, some of them landing on my window ledge...(Three hours later,

on the streets)...The world outside had turned completely gray. Although it was noon, there was very little light...The air was thick and gray, filled with ash. It was difficult to see more than a block ahead. These streets that we walked every single day looked instead like the surface of the moon. The ground was covered in ash more than an inch thick... Occasionally, we came across a church or a public building that was already responding to the crisis. Priests and church staffs were on the sidewalks outside their churches with tables of bottled water and fruit. Poster-board signs were on display, reading "Water, Food, Bathrooms, Telephones, Rest, Prayer." We did not

> take advantage of these offerings, but were moved to see the community reacting so quickly.

Even on the darkest days, *especially* on the darkest days, it is so reassuring to see the gift of community emerge so quickly.

> *E Pluribus Unum*

Sources

INTRODUCTION

Emerson, Ralph Waldo. *The Essays of Ralph Waldo Emerson: Text Established by Alfred R. Ferguson and Jean Ferguson Carr.* Cambridge, Mass.: Belknap Press of Harvard University Press, 1987.

1. A Sense of Community

Hilton, Conrad N. *Be My Guest.* Englewood Cliffs, N.J.: Prentice-Hall, 1957.

2. Life at Lambarene

Cousins, Norman. *Dr. Schweitzer of Lambarene.* New York: Harper & Brothers, 1960.

Anderson, Erica. *The Schweitzer Album: A Portrait in Words and Pictures.* New York: Harper & Row, 1965.

Schweitzer, Albert. *Out of My Life and Thought: An Autobiography.* New York: Henry Holt and Company, 1990.

SECTION I

Hallowell, Edward M. *Connect.* New York: Pantheon Books, 1999.

—— and Michael G. Thompson. *Finding the Heart of the Child: Essays on Children, Families, and Schools.* Washington, D.C.: National Association of Independent Schools, 1993.

Mumford, Lewis. *The City in History: Its Origins, Its Transformations, and Its Prospects.* New York: MJF Books, 1989.

Chekhov, Anton. *The Three Sisters.* New York: Dramatists Play Service, 1984.

Burke, Edmund. *Reflections on the Revolution in France.* New York: Penguin Books, 1968.

3. Life is Dangerous...

Homer. *The Odyssey, with an English Translation by A.T. Murray.* Cambridge, Mass.: Harvard University Press, 1919.

Mumford, Lewis. *The City in History: Its Origins, Its Transformations, and Its Prospects.* New York: MJF Books, 1989.

4. Roseto: The Second Discovery

Wolf, Stewart. *The Roseto Story: An Anatomy of Health.* University of Oklahoma Press, 1979.

Harris, Mark. "The Ties That Bind Are the Ties That Heal." *Vegetarian Times.* Aug 1997.

Ornish, Dean. *Love and Survival: The Scientific Basis for the Healing Power of Intimacy.* New York: HarperCollins, 1998.

5. Part of the Town

New York Times. June 1992.

6. The Statistical Well-Being of Bridges

Birnbaum, Stephen. *Birnbaum's Europe 1988.* Boston: Houghton Mifflin Company, 1987.

Patton, Phil. "To Build a Bridge You Must Cross Troubled Waters." *Smithsonian.* Sept 1996. 84-96.

Toffler, Alvin. *Future Shock*. New York: Random House, 1970.

Ashe, Arthur and Arnold Rampersad. *Days of Grace: A Memoir.* New York: Alfred A. Knopf, Inc., 1993.

7. Birthday Number 101

Abilene Reporter-News. 7 July 2001.

Dawson, George and Richard Glaubman. *Life is So Good*. New York: Random House, 2000.

9. A Brief Business Exchange

Emerson, Ralph Waldo. *The Works of Ralph Waldo Emerson in One Volume: Including the Poems, Philosophic and Inspirational Essays, and Biographical Studies*. New York: Walter J. Black, 1925.

SECTION II

Voggenhuber. *M.C.L. Newsletter*. March/Sept 1990.

Mumford, Lewis. *The City in History: Its Origins, Its Transformations, and Its Prospects*. New York: MJF Books, 1989.

Pinsky, Robert. "Poetry and American Memory." *Atlantic Monthly*. Oct 1999.

Kreidler, John. "Citizens, Start With Culture." *Foundation News and Commentary*. March/April 1996.

10. The Sisterhood of Cities

Kaloyeropoulou, Athena G. *Old Corinth: Diolcos—Isthmia—Lechaeon*. Athens: M. Pechlivanidis & Co. S.A.

Karaim, Reed. "Grand Forks, the City That Won't Give Up." *USA Weekend*. 19-21 Dec 1997.

11. Testimony to the Passing of Time

Phillips, Donald T. *The Founding Fathers on Leadership: Classic Teamwork in Changing Times.* New York: Warner Books, 1997.

Birnbaum, Stephen. *Birnbaum's Europe 1988.* Boston: Houghton Mifflin Company, 1987.

Sandburg, Carl. *Abraham Lincoln: The War Years—IV.* The Sangamon Edition Vol 6. New York: Charles Scribner's Sons, 1941.

Miller, Arthur. *All My Sons.* New York: Chelsea House, 1988.

Cicero, Marcus Tullius, *Pro Publio Sestio*, II, sec. 36.

13. What People Need to Hear

"Now, the Hangover." Time. *15 Jan 1990.*

Yancey, Philip. "Czechoslovakia's Theater of the Absurd." *Christianity Today.* 23 Apr 1990.

Havel, Vaclav. *Summer Meditations.* New York: Vintage Books, 1993.

Demosthenes. *Demosthenes, with an English Translation by J.H. Vince, M.A.* Cambridge, MA: Harvard University Press, 1930.

Pericles. "Funeral Oration" from Thucydides, *The Peloponnesian War.*

14. Taking Up the Cause

Mumford, Lewis. *The City in History: Its Origins, Its Transformations, and Its Prospects.* New York: MJF Books, 1989.

Solon: The Lawmaker of Athens. 23 July 2001. <www.e-classics.com/solon.htm>.

Goldberg, Jim. *Raised by Wolves.* New York: Scalo, 1995.

Strader, Leslie. "Abilene Residents Recognized for Making a Difference." *Abilene Reporter-News Online.* 13 Apr 1997. <http://www.texnews.com/local97/diff041397.html>.

Wilson, Anthony. "Adams Named Point of Light: Retired ACU Dean Honored by Bush for Cleanup Efforts." *Abilene Reporter-News.* 1 July 1992, sec A: 1.

15. The Size of the Canvas

A Brief History of Spoleto Festival USA. *Spoleto Festival USA.* 24 July 2001. *<http://www.spoletousa.org/pageview.asp?id=10>.*

Shapiro, James. *Oberammergau.* New York: Vintage Books, 2001.

16. Mudville: Life in "A Small City"

Giamatti, A. Bartlett. *Take Time for Paradise: Americans and Their Games.* New York: Summit Books, 1989.

Gardner, Martin. *The Annotated Casey at the Bat: A Collection of Ballads About the Mighty Casey.* New York: C.N. Potter, 1967.

Abilene Reporter-News (Associated Press). 15 Aug 1999.

Rampersad, Arnold. *Jackie Robinson: A Biography.* New York: Alfred A. Knopf, 1997.

Robinson, Rachel and Lee Daniels. *Jackie Robinson: An Intimate Portrait.* New York: Harry N. Abrams, 1996.

17. A Sight I Will Not Forget

"Letters to the Editor." *Abilene Reporter-News.* 1997.

SECTION III

Morris, Jan. *Locations.* Toronto: Macfarlane Walter and Ross, 1992.

Putnam, Robert. *Bowling Alone: The Collapse and Revival of American Community.* New York: Simon & Schuster, 2000.

Lewis, Oscar. *Life in a Mexican Village*. Urbana: University of Illinois Press, 1963.

Bradbury, Ray. *Yestermorrow*. Santa Barbara: Joshua Odell Editions, 1991.

18. How to be "At Home in the World"

Lewis, Sinclair. *Main Street*. New York: Penguin, 1980.

Mayeroff, Milton. *On Caring*. New York: Harper & Row, 1971.

19. The Greatest Work of Art Possible

Michener, James. *The Quality of Life*. Greenwich, Conn.: Fawcett Publications, Inc., 1970.

Joyce, William. *Santa Calls*. New York: Scholastic, 1993.

20. Hallmarks of Excellence

Peters, Tom and Robert Waterman. *In Search of Excellence: Lessons from America's Best-run Companies*. New York: Harper & Row, 1982.

Poem used with the permission of Hallmark Cards.

21. A "Courageous" Community

Wright, Jonathan. Telephone Interview.

Drucker, Peter. *Management: Tasks, Responsibilities, Practices*. New York: Harper & Row, 1974.

22. The Symbolic Skyline

Birnbaum, Stephen. *Birnbaum's Europe 1988*. Boston: Houghton Mifflin Company, 1987.

Putnam, Robert. *Bowling Alone: The Collapse and Revival of American Community.* New York: Simon & Schuster, 2000.

Giamatti, A. Bartlett. *Take Time for Paradise: Americans and Their Games.* New York: Summit Books, 1989.

Money, Royce. *Building Stronger Families.* Wheaton, Ill.: Victor Books, 1984.

Michener, James. *This Noble Land: My Vision for America.* New York: Random House, 1996.

23. Knowing What to Look For

Haley, Alex. *Roots.* New York: Dell, 1977.

24. The Pickering Perspective

Shaw, Bernard. *Pygmalion: A Romance in Five Acts.* Harmondsworth: Penguin Books, 1957.

Loewe, Frederick and Alan Jay Lerner. *My Fair Lady: a Musical Play in Two Acts, Based on Pygmalion by Bernard Shaw.* New York: Coward-McCann, 1956.

25. The Meeting Place

Wayman, Norbury L. *St. Louis Union Station and Its Railroads.* St. Louis: Evelyn E. Newman Group, 1986.

Toffler, Alvin. *Future Shock.* New York: Random House, 1970.

26. The Visible (and Invisible) Effects of Time

Peters, Tom and Waterman, Bob. *In Search of Excellence: Lessons from America's Best-run Companies.* New York: Harper & Row, 1982.

Waterman, Bob. *The Renewal Factor: How the Best Get and Keep the Competitive Edge.* Toronto: Bantam Books, 1987.

Gardner, John W. *On Leadership.* New York: Free Press, 1990.

27. Twelve Qualities of Community

Berry, Wendell. *Jayber Crow.* Washington, D.C.: Counterpoint, 2000.

Gaudiani, Claire. *Community of the Future.* San Francisco: Jossey-Bass Publishers, 1998.

Michener, James. *The Quality of Life.* Greenwich, Conn.: Fawcett Publications, Inc., 1970.

Gardner, John. *On Leadership.* New York: Free Press, 1990.

Boswell, James. *Life of Johnson.* London: Oxford University Press, 1957.

Hesselbein, Frances. *Community of the Future.* San Francisco: Jossey-Bass Publishers, 1998.

Kanter, Rosabeth Moss. *World Class.* New York: Simon & Schuster, 1995.

Ruskin, John. *Stones of Venice.* New York: Wiley, 1886.

Bradbury, Ray. *Yestermorrow.* Santa Barbara: Joshua Odell Editions, 1991.

Fukuyama, Francis. *The Great Disruption.* New York: Free Press, 1999.

Havel, Vaclav. *Summer Meditations.* New York: Vintage Books, 1993.

Wiesel, Elie. *And the Sea is Never Full.* New York: Alfred A. Knopf, 1999.

List of Cities